PORTS AND AIRPORTS

getmapping® + HarperCollins*Publishers*

PORTS AND AIRPORTS

AMAZING VIEWS FROM
www.getmapping.com

First published in 2002 by
HarperCollinsPublishers
77–85 Fulham Palace Road
London W6 8JB

The HarperCollins website address is:
www.fireandwater.com

A CIP catalogue record for this book is available from the British Library.

ISBN: 0 00 712279 9

Text by Ian Harrison
Design by Colin Brown
Photographic image processing by Getmapping plc
Colour origination by Colourscan, Singapore
Printed and bound by Editoriale Johnson SpA, Bergamo, Italy

contents

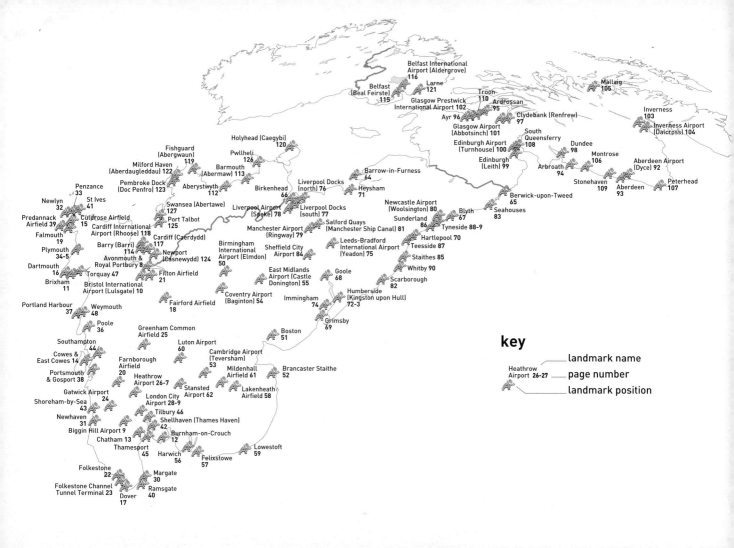

Belfast International
Airport (Aldergrove)
116

Belfast
(Beal Feirste)
115

Larne
121

Glasgow Prestwick
International Airport **102**

Troon
110

Ardrossan
95

Ayr **96**

Clydebank (Renfrew)
97

Glasgow Airport
(Abbotsinch) **101**

South
Queensferry
108

Edinburgh Airport
(Turnhouse) **100**

Edinburgh
(Leith) **99**

Mallaig
105

Inverness
103

Inverness Airport
(Dalcross) **104**

Dundee
98

Montrose
106

Arbroath
94

Stonehaven
109

Aberdeen Airport
(Dyce) **92**

Aberdeen
93

Peterhead
107

Berwick-upon-Tweed
65

Holyhead (Caegybi)
120

Fishguard
(Abergwaun)
119

Pwllheli
126

Milford Haven
(Aberdaugleddau) **122**

Barmouth
(Abermaw) **113**

Pembroke Dock
(Doc Penfro) **123**

Aberystwyth
112

Birkenhead
66

Liverpool Docks
(north) **76**

Barrow-in-Furness
64

Heysham
71

Newcastle Airport
(Woolsington) **80**

Blyth
67

Seahouses
83

Penzance
33

Newlyn
32

St Ives
41

Predannack
Airfield **39**

Culdrose Airfield
15

Falmouth
19

Cardiff International
Airport (Rhoose) **118**

Plymouth
34-5

Barry (Barri)
114

Swansea (Abertawe)
127

Port Talbot
125

Cardiff (Caerdydd)
117

Liverpool Airport
(Speke) **78**

Liverpool Docks
(south) **77**

Salford Quays
(Manchester Ship Canal) **81**

Sunderland
86

Tyneside **88-9**

Hartlepool **70**

Teesside **87**

Manchester Airport
(Ringway) **79**

Sheffield City
Airport **84**

Leeds-Bradford
International Airport
(Yeadon) **75**

Staithes **85**

Whitby **90**

Dartmouth
16

Newport
(Casnewydd) **124**

Avonmouth &
Royal Portbury **8**

Birmingham
International
Airport (Elmdon)
50

East Midlands
Airport (Castle
Donington) **55**

Goole
68

Scarborough
82

Brixham
11

Torquay **47**

Filton Airfield
21

Bristol International
Airport (Lulsgate) **10**

Humberside
(Kingston upon Hull)
72-3

Portland Harbour
37

Weymouth
48

Poole
36

Coventry Airport
(Baginton) **54**

Fairford Airfield
18

Immingham
74

Grimsby
69

Boston
51

Southampton
44

Greenham Common
Airfield **25**

Luton Airport
60

Cambridge Airport
(Teversham)
53

Brancaster Staithe
52

Cowes &
East Cowes **14**

Portsmouth
& Gosport **38**

Farnborough
Airfield
20

Heathrow
Airport **26-7**

Mildenhall
Airfield **61**

Gatwick Airport
24

Shoreham-by-Sea
43

Stansted
Airport **62**

London City
Airport **28-9**

Lakenheath
Airfield **58**

Newhaven
31

Biggin Hill Airport **9**

Chatham **13**

Tilbury **46**

Shellhaven (Thames Haven)
42

Lowestoft
59

Thamesport
45

Burnham-on-Crouch
12

Folkestone
22

Harwich
56

Felixstowe
57

Folkestone Channel
Tunnel Terminal **23**

Dover
17

Margate
30

Ramsgate
40

key

the south

Avonmouth and Royal Portbury
Avon

1. Industrial ports
2. United Nations carrier code: GB BRS
3. Vessel capacity: 170 m length, 40,000 dwt (Avonmouth)/300 m length, 130,000 dwt (Royal Portbury)
4. Goods handled: Dry bulks, forest products, vehicles, refined petroleum
5. Origin of name: Stands at the mouth of the River Avon (Avon from the Celtic "river")

England Photographic Atlas: Page 97, H3

Authority: Bristol Port Company
Tel: (0117) 982 0000

There are two ports at the mouth of the River Avon, both of which owe their existence to the growing size of cargo ships. Avonmouth, to the north of the river, was opened in 1880 to accommodate ships that were too large to travel upriver to the existing port of Bristol, while Royal Portbury, to the south, was opened a century later to receive ships that were too large for Avonmouth.

Biggin Hill Airport
Kent, 5.5m e-se of Croydon

1. Opened: 1917
2. Air transport movements (2000): 1,323
3. Passengers (2000): 6,168
4. Runways: 03/21 (1,808 m) & 11/29 (816 m)
5. Radio frequencies (MHz): 134.8 (tower)/129.4 (approach)

England Photographic Atlas: Page 195, E4

Operated by: Regional Airports Ltd
Tel: (01959) 571111

Biggin Hill is most famous as "the Battle of Britain airfield", and deservedly so – by the middle of 1943 aircraft based at Biggin Hill had destroyed 1,000 enemy planes, a record that was never beaten. The main runway was extended in 1957 to accommodate jet aircraft but only two years later the RAF ceased flying from Biggin Hill, since when the airfield has been used by light aircraft and executive flights, with scheduled services to northern France. The number of air transport movements is far outnumbered by nearly 100,000 club and private flights each year.

Bristol International Airport (Lulsgate)
7m s-w of Bristol, Avon

1. Opened: RAF 1939, Civil 1957
2. Air transport movements (2000): 36,185
3. Passengers (2000): 2,142,626
4. Runway: 09/27 (2,011 m)
5. Radio frequencies (MHz): 133.85
   (tower)/128.55 (approach)

England Photographic Atlas: Page 86, A2

Operated by: Bristol Airport plc
Tel: 0870 1212 747

Lulsgate was originally due to be a nightfighter base called Broadfield Down, but instead became a Tiger Moth flying school named Lulsgate Bottom. Built in 1939 for the Air Ministry, it was used only by gliders immediately after the war and was officially opened as the new Bristol Airport on 1st May 1957. Today, in addition to operating as a passenger airport, Lulsgate is also used by Post Office mail flights.

Brixham
Devon

1. Fishing port
2. United Nations carrier code: GB BRX
3. Facilities: Ice plant, Prince William Quay Marina (450 berths)
4. Goods handled: Fishing boats, leisure craft
5. Origin of name: Old English "Brioc's village"

England Photographic Atlas: Page 31, H2

Authority: Torbay Borough Council
Tel: (01803) 296244

It is said that when William of Orange landed at Brixham in 1688 to claim the English crown, his ship ran aground in the harbour and one of the town's fishermen waded out to carry the future King William III ashore – William's proclamation that "the liberties of England I will maintain" was adopted by the town as its motto. Henry Francis Lyte, who was the first vicar of All Saints Church in Lower Brixham, wrote "Abide With Me" at Berry Head House after watching the sun set over Tor Bay in 1847, shortly before he died. But even more than Glorious Revolutions and football anthems, Brixham is famous for its fishing fleet, pioneers of deep-sea trawling that made 19th century Brixham "the great fishery of the West".

Burnham-on-Crouch
Essex

1. Sailing centre and port
2. United Nations carrier code: GB 149 (Baltic Wharf)
3. Vessel capacity: 6.5 m draught (harbour)/7.5 m draught (Baltic Wharf)
4. Goods handled: Leisure craft (harbour)/Forest products, steel (Baltic Wharf)
5. Origin of name: Old English "homestead on the stream by the Crouch" (stands on the Crouch estuary)

England Photographic Atlas: Page 268, B2

Authority: Crouch Harbour Authority
Tel: (01621) 783602

Burnham-on-Crouch is a picturesque town with an undeniably maritime air – colour-washed cottages along the Quay, smuggler's inns and up to 2,000 yachts bobbing in the harbour, which is home to 21 yacht clubs, boat-builders' yards and marinas. To the west of the harbour on the south bank of the River Crouch is Burnham's commercial dock, the Baltic Wharf.

Chatham
Kent

1. Former naval base (16th century–1984)
2. United Nations carrier code: GB CTM
3. Vessel capacity: 4.93 m draught, 145 m length
4. Goods handled: Steel, wire mesh, aggregates, vehicles, general cargo, forest products
5. Origin of name: Celtic and Old English "village by the wood"

England Photographic Atlas: Page 248, C6

Authority: Medway Ports
Tel: (01634) 814936

The Royal Dockyard at Chatham was founded by Henry VIII when he formally established a permanent navy. The port was enlarged by Elizabeth I and modernized by Charles II, by whose reign it had become the country's largest naval base. Charles Dickens's father worked for the Navy Pay Office and was transferred to Chatham when Dickens was five; from 1817–21 they lived at No 2 (now No 11) Ordnance Terrace. The 80 acres of dockyards were closed in 1984 and re-opened the following year as an industrial estate, marina and museum, part of the dockyard being preserved as Chatham Historic Dockyard.

13

Cowes and East Cowes
Isle of Wight

1. Seaport & resort
2. United Nations carrier code: GB COW
3. Vessel capacity: 4.7 m draught, 85 m length
4. Goods handled: Roadstone, aggregates,
   fuel oil, timber, grain, car ferries
5. Origin of name: From two sandbanks at
   the mouth of the River Medina,
   known as 'The Cows'

England Photographic Atlas: Page 119, H6

Authority: Cowes Harbour Commissioners
Tel: (01983) 293952

The towns of Cowes and East Cowes, separated by the
River Medina, are quite distinct entities. East Cowes, the
more industrial, is 'the cradle and headquarters of the
hovercraft industry' (Cockerell's hovercraft made its first
test runs from here), while Cowes itself is the
undisputed yachting capital of Britain, home of the Royal
Yacht Squadron which is housed in Cowes Castle. This
exclusive sailing club was formed in Cowes as the Yacht
Club in 1815. The Prince Regent, later George IV,
became a member in 1818 and the name was
subsequently changed to the Royal Yacht Club and later,
by royal command, to the Royal Yacht Squadron. Every
August, Cowes plays host to the international yachting
festival known as Cowes Week.

Culdrose Airfield
Helston, Cornwall

1. Opened: 1947
2. Service: RN (HMS Seahawk)
3. ICAO code: EGDR
4. Runways: 12/30 (1,830 m), 07/25 (1,042 m) & 18/36 (1,051 m)

England Photographic Atlas: Page 19, E6

Tel: (01326) 574121

During the 1950s, Culdrose became the Navy's main helicopter training base and is now home to several squadrons of Merlins and Sea Kings involved in rescue, airborne early warning and anti-submarine roles. The airfield is also host to the Navy's Culdrose Gliding Club.

15

Dartmouth
Devon

1. Seaport
2. United Nations carrier code: GB DTM
3. Vessel capacity: 8.3 m draught, 152 m length, 10,000 dwt
4. Goods handled: Fish, freight, leisure craft
5. Origin of name: Stands at the mouth of the River Dart (Dart from Celtic "river beside which oak trees grow")

England Photographic Atlas: Page 31, G3

Port operated by: Dart Harbour & Navigation Authority
Tel: (01803) 832337

Since Norman times Dartmouth has thrived due to its deep-water harbour. Fleets embarked from here in the 12th century for the Second and Third Crusades, and nearly 800 years later the Allied fleet sailed from Dartmouth to Utah beach for the Normandy landings. By the late 14th century the port was renowned enough for local ship-owner John Hawley to serve as the model for Chaucer's Shipman – "For aught I woote, he was of Dertemouthe" – and during the reign of Elizabeth I 'Dertemouthe' was used by sailors and explorers including Sir Francis Drake, John Davis and Sir Walter Raleigh's half-brother, Sir Humphrey Gilbert, whose house overlooking the Dart was later rebuilt for Agatha Christie. Since 1905, Dartmouth has been the home of the Britannia Royal Naval College, seen to the top left of the picture.

Dover
Kent

1. Seaport & market town
2. United Nations carrier code: GB DVR
3. Traffic (per annum): c. 20 m passengers, 3 m tourist cars, 1.5 m HGVs, 0.15 m coaches
4. Goods handled: Ferry passengers, ro-ro freight, fresh fruit and vegetables, ballast
5. Origin of name: Celtic (place on the) "waters" or "stream"

England Photographic Atlas: Page 183, E4

Authority: Dover Harbour Board
Tel: (01304) 240400

The Romans used "Dubris" as a port because a sand and shingle bank formed by the outfall of the River Dour provided a natural harbour. Being Britain's closest point to mainland Europe, Dover has witnessed some historic channel crossings in addition to the regular ferry services. In 1875 Captain Matthew Webb left Dover to become the first person to swim the Channel without a lifejacket, and in 1909 Louis Blériot landed here after making the first cross-Channel flight. Dover is also famous for its 12th-century castle and, of course, for its White Cliffs.

Fairford Airfield
2m s of Fairford, Gloucestershire

1. Opened: 1944
2. Service: USAF
3. ICAO code: EGVA
4. Runway: 09/27 (3,047 m)

England Photographic Atlas: Page 113, E4

Tel: (01285) 714000

Fairford opened under the control of Bomber Command but was almost immediately transferred to Transport Command, whose gliders played an important role over Normandy and Arnhem during World War II. From 1950 until 1964, the base was under the control of the US Air Force (USAF), during which time the runway was lengthened. There was then a series of temporary residents including the Red Arrows and Concorde, before Fairford took on its current role as a stand-by base for the USAF. Fairford also hosts the annual Royal International Air Tattoo each July on behalf of the RAF Benevolent Fund.

Falmouth
Cornwall

1. Port
2. United Nations carrier code: GB FAL
3. Vessel capacity: 460,000 dwt
4. Industries: Ship-repairing, marine engineering
5. Origin of name: Stands at the mouth of the River Fal

England Photographic Atlas: Page 20, C4

Authority: Falmouth Harbour Commissioners
Tel: (01326) 211376

It was Sir Walter Raleigh who recognised the potential of Falmouth as a port, and the family of his friend Sir Peter Killigrew who transformed the small fishing village into a major port by building a deep-water harbour. In 1689 Falmouth became the base of the Falmouth Packets, carrying trans-Atlantic mail; in the 19th century the arrival of the railways led to the town's development as a resort, and in the 20th century a dry dock was established, capable of handling tankers of up to 90,000 tons.

Farnborough Airfield
Farnborough, Hampshire

1. Opened: 1905
2. Operator: TAG Aviation
3. ICAO code: EGLF
4. Runways: 09/27 (2,360 m), 18/36 & 24/06 now used as taxiways B & D
5. Radio frequencies (MHz): 122.5 (tower)/134.35 (approach)

England Photographic Atlas:
Page 165, G1

Flying has taken place at Farnborough since the Army's Balloon Equipment Store relocated here in 1905 to become HM Balloon Factory. Civilian balloonist Samuel Cody made Britain's first powered flight in 1908 at Farnborough, the balloon factory became the Royal Aircraft Establishment (now part of the Defence Evaluation & Research Agency). The Royal Flying Corps was formed here in 1912, amalgamating in 1918 with the Royal Naval Air Service to become the Royal Air Force. More recently Farnborough has been involved in the development of Whittle's jet engine, Concorde, and the Thrust Supersonic Car, and since 1948 the airfield has hosted what is now the biennial Farnborough International Airshow.

Filton Airfield

4m n of Bristol, Avon

1. Opened: 1910
2. Operator: British Aerospace (Bae)
3. Use: Airbus freighter conversions
4. Runways: 09/27 (2,436 m) & 03/21 (1,231 m, disused)
5. Radio frequencies (MHz): 132.35 (tower)/122.725 (approach)

England Photographic Atlas: Page 98, D2
Tel: (0117) 969 3831

An aircraft factory opened at Filton in 1910, when planes took off from "the top of the hill". It wasn't until the late 1920s that a grass strip was laid out on the site of the present runway, which was upgraded to concrete during the 1940s. The new runway was a massive 90 metres wide to accommodate the wide undercarriage of the Brabazon – most modern planes can take off and land on runways of half that width. In April 1969 Concorde 002, the British-built prototype, made a 20-minute flight from Filton, piloted by Brian Trubshaw, who described it as a "wizard flight". Filton was pipped at the post in the history-making stakes by Toulouse, where Concorde 001 made its maiden flight a month earlier.

Folkestone
Kent

1. Port & holiday resort
2. United Nations carrier code: GB FOL
3. Vessel capacity: 5.0 m draught, 130 m length
4. Goods handled: Cross-channel ferries, fishing
5. Origin of name: Old English, either "Folca's stone" or "people's stone" (the stone marking a meeting-place)

England Photographic Atlas: Page 181, F4

Authority: Folkestone Properties Ltd
Tel: (01303) 220544

Folkestone seems to provoke extreme reactions in its visitors, with descriptions ranging from "one of the most lovable of Britain's seaside resorts, and one of the prettiest" to "a drab and utterly missable introduction to this swathe of coast". Charles Dickens was more ambiguous. He visited in 1855 and wrote of climbing "a precipitous cliff in a lonely spot overhanging the wild sea-beach", which could be seen as praise or damnation, depending on one's outlook.

Folkestone Channel Tunnel Terminal
Kent

1. Opened: 1994
2. Length of tunnel: 50 km (39 km undersea section 40 m below sea bed)
3. Capacity: 120 cars and 12 coaches per Shuttle
4. Traffic (2001): c. 2.5 m cars, 1.2 m trucks, 0.075 m coaches
5. Freight handled (2001): 2,477,432 tonnes

England Photographic Atlas: Page 180, D4
Operated by: Eurotunnel (Le Shuttle) Tel: 0870 535 3535

The idea of a Channel Tunnel was first envisioned 200 years ago, after the Treaty of Amiens in 1802. Plans were drawn up for two tunnels meeting at an artificial island built mid-Channel, with stabling facilities for the horses that drew the coaches, but the project was scuppered by the fact that war broke out again a year later and Napoleon began planning an invasion of England. After two false starts during the 19th century, it was 1986 before Prime Minister Margaret Thatcher and President Mitterand signed the Treaty of Canterbury and the project at last got under way. Work began in 1987 and the tunnel was officially opened in May 1994, when the Queen and President Mitterand travelled on Le Shuttle in the Queen's Rolls-Royce.

23

Gatwick Airport
28m s of London

1. Licensed for flying: 1930 (officially opened 1936)
2. Air transport movements (2000): 252,773
3. Passengers (2000): 32,068,540
4. Runways: 08R/26L (3,316 m) & 08L/26R (2,565 m)
5. Radio frequencies (MHz): 124.225 (tower)/126.825 (approach)

England Photographic Atlas: Page 169, H6

Operated by: British Airports Authority
Tel: 0870 000 2468

Gatwick's first terminal building was known as the Beehive because of the distinctive shape of its up-to-the-minute 1930s design. Civilian flying was suspended during the war, during which military users included Mustangs undertaking photo-reconnaissance vital to the D-Day landings. After the war, Gatwick was expanded, having been earmarked as London's second airport, and in June 1958 it was re-opened by HM The Queen and Prince Philip. The airport was massively enlarged in the 1970s, and again in the 1990s with an £80m redevelopment plan, and now covers an area of 1,876 acres.

Greenham Common Airfield
2m s of Thatcham, Berkshire

1. Opened: 1941
2. Service: RAF 1941–53, USAF 1953–92, Greenham Common Trust 1997 onwards
3. Use: Business park, housing, school, wildlife trust, parks
4. Runway: 3,048 m with parallel taxiways
5. Historic events: Continuous peace protest, 1981–91

England Photographic Atlas: Page 186, A2

Site owned by: Greenham Common Trust
Tel: (01635) 817444

The use of Greenham Common as an airbase was controversial from the start, being built on ancient common land that was appropriated by the military in 1941 under emergency wartime powers. The base was deactivated and recommissioned twice before the arrival of 96 Cruise Missiles in 1980. The ensuing peace protest, a decade-long women's vigil at the perimeter fence, kept Greenham Common in the headlines until the last of the missiles was removed in March 1991. When the base was declared redundant for military purposes, local people, concerned that it would be sold to developers, formed the Greenham Common Trust, bought the former airbase in 1997 and set up facilities there for the benefit of the local community.

Heathrow Airport
14m w of London

1. Opened: Fairey 1929, Civil 1946
2. Air transport movements (2000): 460,476
3. Passengers (2000): 64,620,286
4. Runways: 09R/27L (3,658 m), 09L/27R (3,902 m) & 05/23 (1,966 m)
5. Radio frequencies (MHz): 118.7, 118.5 (tower)/119.725, 120.4, 134.975 (approach)

England Photographic Atlas: Page 217, G4

Operated by: British Airports Authority
Tel: 0870 000 0123

When the first aerodrome was built at Heathrow by Richard Fairey in 1929, on land bought from the vicar of Harmondsworth, local residents were placated by the fact that it was a test site and therefore there would be very few flights! During the Second World War the Air Ministry decided to develop Heathrow with the long term view of using it as a civil airport after the war, and used emergency wartime powers for the compulsory purchase of land which included Fairey's aerodrome. The civilian airport opened in 1946 and, just over half a century later, Heathrow is the world's busiest passenger airport and second biggest cargo airport, with plans for a fifth terminal handling an extra 30 million passengers every year.

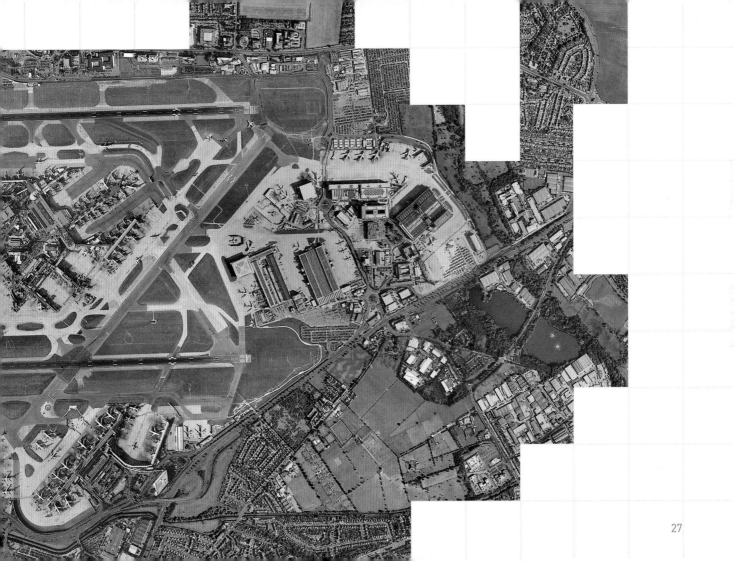

London City Airport
Docklands, east London

1. Opened: 1987
2. Air transport movements (2000): 50,049
3. Passengers (2000): 1,583,843
4. Runway: 10/28 (1,199 m)
5. Radio frequencies (MHz): 118.075, 127.95 (tower)/132.7 (approach)

England Photographic Atlas: Page 238, B4

Operated by: London City Airport Ltd
Tel: (020) 7646 0000

The runway of London City Airport lies on what was once the bustling centre quay between the Royal Albert and King George V docks, both at one time crowded with ships waiting to unload. The first meeting between the developers, Mowlem Construction, and the London Docklands Development Corporation took place early in 1981, but work didn't begin until April 1986 after a public inquiry over planning permission, and wrangling between the Port of London Authority and the LDDC over ownership of the freehold. Commercial services began on 26th October 1987 and the airport was officially opened by the Queen just over a week later on 5th November. In 1992 the runway was lengthened to accommodate larger aircraft, and in 1998 the maximum permitted number of flights was doubled, rising to 73,000.

Margate
Kent

1. Seaside resort
2. Visitors to tourist office (2001): 48,410
3. Features: Long promenade with pier and lido
4. Industries: Tourism, textiles, scientific instruments
5. Origin of name: Old English "sea gate" (possibly from a gap in the cliffs leading to the sea)

England Photographic Atlas: Page 207, G2

Tourist office tel: (01843) 583334

Thomas Gray described Margate as "Bartholomew Fair by the Seaside", Oscar Wilde called it "the nom-de-plume of Ramsgate", and a modern guide refers to it as "Blackpool in Kent". Judging by these epithets, Margate has been going downhill since the mid-18th century when it was pioneering the use of bathing machines, although at its peak popularity in the mid-19th century, thousands of Londoners were travelling down the Thames to disembark at Margate's pier, said to be the forerunner of all other seaside piers.

Newhaven
East Sussex

1. Port
2. United Nations carrier code: GB NHV
3. Vessel capacity: 8.5 m draught, 165 m length
4. Goods handled: Ferry passengers, fruit, vegetables, meat, sand, ballast, steel
5. Origin of name: Old English "new harbour"

England Photographic Atlas: Page 131, G5

Authority: Newhaven Port & Properties Ltd
Tel: (01273) 514131

There are conflicting ideas as to why the "new harbour" was built. One theory is that it was part of a 16th-century scheme to drain the marshland of the Ouse valley, another that a storm in 1579 altered the course of the river which until then had flowed into the Channel at Seaford. With the river's change of course the former village of Meeching became Newhaven because it was just that – a new haven, or harbour. In 1878 the London, Brighton & South Coast Railway financed deep water quays at the harbour to improve the company's Newhaven-Dieppe ferry service, tripling the passenger figures in 30 years. The 900 m curving stone jetty was completed in 1891 with an iron lighthouse at its head that still watches the Dieppe ferry come and go.

Newlyn
Cornwall

1. Seaport
2. United Nations carrier code: GB NYL
3. Vessel capacity: 5.8 m draught, 103 m length
4. Goods handled: Primarily fish (c. 12,000 t/year)
5. Origin of name: Old Cornish, "harbour for a fleet of boats"

England Photographic Atlas: Page 13, E3

Authority: Newlyn Pier & Harbour Commission
Tel: (01736) 362523

The Ordnance Survey relates heights in Britain to mean sea level at Newlyn, a town which gave its name to the Newlyn School of artists (1880–90), which included Dame Laura Knight, Frank Bramley and Stanhope Forbes.

Penzance
Cornwall

1. Seaport & resort
2. United Nations carrier code: GB PEN
3. Vessel capacity: 4.5 m draught, 65 m length, 1,800 dwt
4. Goods handled: General cargo, fish (c. 10,000 t/year)
5. Origin of name: Old Cornish "holy headland"

England Photographic Atlas: Page 13, E2

Authority: Penwith District Council
Tel: (01736) 366133

Known as the Cornish Riviera, Penzance has a climate so mild that palm trees thrive in the Morrab Gardens on the seafront (morrab is the Cornish word for sea-shore). The 17th-century Union Hotel is where news of Nelson's victory and death at Trafalgar was first announced. Sir Humphry Davy, the inventor of the miner's safety lamp, was born in Penzance in 1778.

Plymouth Hoe is immortalized in legend as the place where Sir Francis Drake played bowls in 1588 as the Spanish Armada approached. At that time, Plymouth was England's foremost port, exceeding even London in its volume of trade. Hawkins, Raleigh, Frobisher, Captain Cook and Sir Francis Chichester are among the maritime heroes to have sailed from this historic port, and it was from here that the Pilgrim Fathers set sail in the Mayflower in 1620, founding Plymouth, Massachusetts on their arrival in the New World. The modern city was formed by the amalgamation of the three towns of Stonehouse, Devonport and Plymouth, and has three mercantile harbours: Sutton Harbour, whose facilities include a 350-berth yacht marina; Millbay Docks, operated by Associated British Ports and Cattewater Harbour.

Plymouth
Devon

1. Seaport (three mercantile harbours & naval dockyard)
2. United Nations carrier code: GB PLY
3. Vessel capacity: 8.5 m draught, 200 m length
4. Goods handled: Ro-ro freight, general cargo, ferry and cruise passengers (Devonport naval dockyard used for refitting nuclear submarines)
5. Origin of name: Stands at the mouth of the River Plym (Plym from Old English "plum-tree farm")

England Photographic Atlas: Page 29, E4

Harbours operated by: Associated British Ports, Cattewater Harbour Authority, Sutton Harbour Co, MOD

Poole
Dorset

1. Industrial town & port
2. United Nations carrier code: GB POO
3. Vessel capacity: 5.5 m draught, 160 m length
4. Traffic (per annum): c. 0.75 m t cargo, 0.85 m passengers, 0.25 m passenger vehicles, 0.09 m freight vehicles
5. Origin of name: Old English "pool" (describing the natural harbour)

England Photographic Atlas: Page 52, A3

Authority: Poole Harbour Commissioners
Tel: (01202) 440200

The name "Pole" was first recorded in 1183 and the town, now Dorset's largest, grew to prominence during the 13th century, partly through the shipment of the local Purbeck marble and partly through the activities of smugglers, pirates and fishermen. By the 18th century, Poole was attracting the lion's share of trade with Newfoundland – ships would depart in the spring carrying supplies for the colonists, then fish the Newfoundland waters during the summer, trading the dried fish in Spain and Portugal on the way home and finally returning to Poole with wine and other imports.

Portland Harbour
Dorset

1. Man-made harbour
2. United Nations carrier code: GB PTL
3. Vessel capacity: 15 m draught, 600 m length (inner breakwater berth)
4. Goods handled: Cruise passengers, fertiliser, stone, grain, cable, liquid bulk, aggregates
5. Origin of name: Old English 'estate by the harbour'

England Photographic Atlas: Page 46, D5

Port authority: Portland Port Ltd Tel: (01305) 824044

The Isle of Portland, dubbed Portland "the Gibraltar of Wessex" by Thomas Hardy, is scarred with quarries yielding the famous Portland Stone, sought after since Christopher Wren used it to build St Paul's Cathedral. This hard limestone was also used to build the 1,900 m breakwater that encloses Portland Harbour, Britain's largest man-made harbour and home to a major naval base from 1845–1995.

Portsmouth and Gosport
Hampshire

1. City & naval port
2. United Nations carrier code: GB PME
3. Vessel capacity: 7 m draught, 180 m length
4. Goods handled: Ferries, fruit, fish, general cargo
5. Origin of name: Old English "port at the harbour mouth"/Old English "goose market"

England Photographic Atlas:
Page 122-123

Authority: Portsmouth Commercial Port
(Portsmouth City Council)
Tel: (023) 9229 7395

Superstar status was already a phenomenon by the turn of the 19th century – when Nelson left his hotel on Portsmouth High Street to join the Victory on 14th September 1805, a few weeks before his death at the Battle of Trafalgar, he had to leave by the back staircase to avoid the crowd of people waiting outside to catch a glimpse of the national hero. And the port has played host to other celebrities: engineer and ship builder Isambard Kingdom Brunel was born in Portsmouth in 1806, Charles Dickens was born here in 1812 (his father worked for the Navy), the 15 year-old HG Wells was a draper's assistant in the town, and Sir Arthur Conan Doyle practised medicine in Southsea.

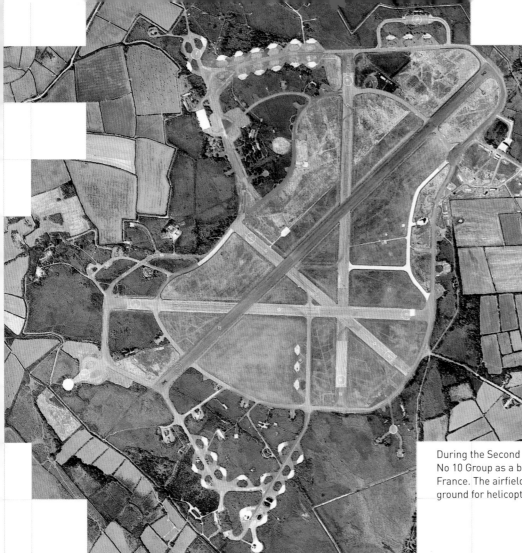

Predannack Airfield
5m s of Culdrose, Cornwall

1. Opened: WWII
2. Service: RN
3. ICAO code: EGDO
4. Runways: Eight, main
   runway 05/23 (5,950 ft)

England Photographic Atlas:
Page 16, C4

Tel: (01326) 574121 xtn 2319

During the Second World War, Predannack was used by
No 10 Group as a base for bombing missions into
France. The airfield is now used as a relief landing
ground for helicopters based at Culdrose.

Ramsgate
Kent

1. Seaside resort & port
2. United Nations carrier code: GB RMG
3. Vessel capacity: 7 m draught, 165 m length
4. Industries: Tourism, cross-channel ferries, fishing, yachting
5. Origin of name: Old English "Hraefn's gap" (from a gap in the cliffs)

England Photographic Atlas: Page 207, H5

Authority: Thanet District Council
Tel: (01843) 592277

Jane Austen visited Ramsgate at the turn of the 19th century, and the town appears in both Mansfield Park (1813) and Pride and Prejudice (1814). Another influential visitor was George IV, who popularized the town as a resort. The Royal Harbour shelters fishing boats, a large marina, and catamarans and ferries to and from Ostend.

St Ives
Cornwall

1. Fishing port & resort
2. Visitors to tourist office (2001): 124,246
3. Features: Tate Gallery, Barbara Hepworth Museum
4. Industries: Tourism, fishing
5. Origin of name: Saint Ya (recorded as "Sancta Ya" in 1284)

England Photographic Atlas: Page 15, G2

Tourist office tel: (01736) 796297

The waters off St Ives, once famous for pilchards, were so well stocked during the 19th century that sixteen and a half million fish are recorded as having been caught in one net in a single day in 1868, and it was said that sometimes the smell of fish was so strong that it stopped the church clock! Virginia Woolf spent her summers here as a child and Godrevy Lighthouse, across the bay from St Ives, is thought to be the setting for her novel "To The Lighthouse".

Shellhaven (aka Thames Haven)
Essex

1. Oil and liquid bulk terminal
2. United Nations carrier code: GB LON
3. Vessel capacity: 14.6 m draught, 355 m length
4. Goods handled: Oil, bitumen, aviation fuel, liquid bulk, petroleum products
5. Origin of name: "Shell harbour" (from the Shell oil company)/"Thames harbour" (Thames from Celtic "river" or "dark one")

England Photographic Atlas: Page 248, B2

Authority: Port of London Authority (PLA)
Tel: (020) 7743 7900

Currently known officially as Thames Haven, this huge oil terminal and storage facility was developed by the Shell oil company and is popularly known by its former name of Shellhaven. It occupies 100 acres on the eastern edge of the site at Coryton, bordering the river inlet, and is now owned and operated by BP. Shell has closed its oil terminals at Shellhaven but still operates part of the site for handling bitumen and aviation products. Shell and P&O Ports have submitted plans to redevelop the entire site as a massive new container port to be known as London Gateway.

Shoreham-by-Sea
West Sussex

1. Port & sailing resort
2. United Nations carrier code: GB SHO
3. Vessel capacity: 6.7 m draught, 105.9 m length (in lock)
4. Industries: Sailing, container port
5. Origin of name: Old English "homestead by a slope"; suffix added 19th century

England Photographic Atlas: Page 129, F5

Authority: Shoreham Port Authority
Tel: (01273) 598100

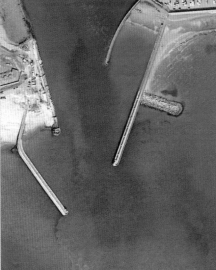

Shoreham has the feel of three separate towns, with the estuary of the River Adur providing sheltered waters for canoeists and yachtsmen, a popular beach to the west of the harbour mouth, and the busy container port to the east. The town takes its name not from the shore but from the Old English word for slope: the original settlement was on the slopes of the South Downs and is now known as Old Shoreham – the part of the town that spread towards the coast was at first known as New Shoreham, with the suffix "by-Sea" added in the 19th century when coastal resorts were becoming popular.

Southampton
Hampshire

1. Seaport
2. United Nations carrier code: GB SOU
3. Vessel capacity: 422,000 dwt
4. Goods handled: Containers, ro-ro vehicles, cruise passengers, fresh produce, grain, liquid and dry bulks (c. 34m t/year)
5. Origin of name: Old English "riverside farmstead", the "south" added later (the county name Hampshire is derived from the city's earlier name of Hamtun)

England Photographic Atlas: Page 139, F6

Authority: Associated British Ports
Tel: (020) 7430 1177

The ancient port of Southampton grew to prominence in the second half of the 19th century with the arrival of the railway and the sudden growth in the size of passenger liners. The town also took over from Falmouth (p. 19) as a mail port, with the Royal Mail and the Union-Castle steamship line using it as their main port – soon afterwards, Cunard made Southampton its base, all of which led to the building of deep-water quays, dry docks, basins, and facilities for ship-building and repairing. Modern Southampton includes the UK's second largest container terminal, run jointly by P&O and Associated British Ports.

Thamesport
Isle of Grain, Kent

1. Container port
2. United Nations carrier code: GB THP
3. Vessel capacity: 13.5 m draught, 650 m length
4. Goods handled: Bitumen, jet fuel, aggregate, containers
5. Origin of name: Port on the River Thames

England Photographic Atlas: Page 249, G4

Authority: Thamesport (London) Ltd (member of the Hutchison Port Holdings Group) Tel: (01634) 271511

Thamesport is Europe's fastest growing container port, just a decade old and already the UK's third largest, with computerized cranes handling container cargo from up to 100 ships per month. This purpose-built port is located on the site of a former oil refinery on the Isle of Grain, perfectly placed where the mouth of the river Medway meets the mouth of the Thames, with brownfield land alongside for future development as the port continues to grow.

45

Tilbury
Essex

1. Industrial town & container port
2. United Nations carrier code: GB TIL
3. Vessel capacity: 12.5 m draught, 304 m length
4. Goods handled: Forest products, grain, containers, general cargo (c. 9.4m t/year)
5. Origin of name: Old English "Tila's stronghold"

England Photographic Atlas:
Page 247, F4

Port operated by: Port of Tilbury
London Limited
Tel: (01375) 852200

Tilbury occupied an important strategic position on the Thames long before the port was built here: the name itself, first recorded in the 8th century, refers to a stronghold or fortified place, and a more modern fortress, Tilbury Fort, was built here 1682 to prevent the Dutch or French from entering London via the Thames. The Port of Tilbury, constructed in 1888 to the west of the fort, covers an area of 800 acres. It is a multi-purpose port handling in excess of 3000 shipping movements per year, and includes the Northfleet Hope Terminal (to the west of the site), London's largest container terminal.

Torquay
Devon

1. Resort & port
2. United Nations carrier code: GB TOR
3. Vessel capacity: 3 m draught, 90 m length
4. Goods handled: Leisure craft (Torquay Marina 475 berths)
5. Origin of name: Old and Middle English "quay near the rocky hill"

England Photographic Atlas: Page 31, H1

Authority: Torbay Borough Council
Tel: (01803) 296244

Torquay goes one further than Penzance (which bills itself the Cornish Riviera) by claiming the title "English Riviera" – and it certainly looks the part, with its ostentatious marina, sub-tropical vegetation and mini-corniche. The town's story began with the monks of Torre Abbey, who built a quay on the north side of Tor Bay, allowing the settlement to thrive and providing it with a new name. From the 19th century onwards, Torquay transformed itself from a fishing village into a resort among whose early visitors was Tennyson, who stayed here in 1838 and described Torquay as "the loveliest sea-village in England".

Weymouth
Dorset

1. Seaport & resort
2. United Nations carrier code: GB WEY
3. Vessel capacity: 5.2 m draught, 130 m length
4. Goods handled: Car ferries, ro-ro general cargo, wine, fertilisers, aggregates, cement (freight c. 50,000 t/year)
5. Origin of name: Stands at the mouth of the River Wey (Wey possibly from the Celtic "mover")

England Photographic Atlas: Page 46, D4

Authority: Weymouth & Portland Borough Council
Tel: (01305) 206278

Henry VIII used Weymouth as a naval base and George III popularized it as a bathing resort, but the town had been a port for centuries before either of them discovered it, making some historic imports and exports – Weymouth was the first place in England to suffer from the Black Death in 1348 and, in 1628, saw the departure of Dorchester-born John Endecott for America, where he founded Salem, Massachusetts.

east anglia and the midlands

Birmingham International Airport (Elmdon)
6m e-se of Birmingham, West Midlands

1. Officially opened: 8th July 1936
2. Air transport movements (2000): 108,972
3. Passengers (2000): 7,596,893
4. Runways: 15/33 (2,605 m) & 06/24 (1,315 m)
5. Radio frequencies (MHz): 118.3 (tower)/118.05 (approach)

England Photographic Atlas: Page 433, G3

Operated by: Birmingham International Airport plc
Tel: (0121) 767 5511

Only three years after it was opened by the Duchess of Kent, Birmingham Airport was commandeered by the Air Ministry for the duration of the Second World War. A Flying Training School was established here, using Tiger Moths, and Elmdon was also used as a flight test centre for Stirlings and Lancasters built by Austin at Longbridge. Since the war the airport has grown rapidly, with an extension to the terminal opened by the Duchess of Kent in 1961, runway and terminal extensions in 1967, an entirely new terminal building opened by HM The Queen and Prince Philip in 1984, and a satellite terminal under construction at the turn of the millennium.

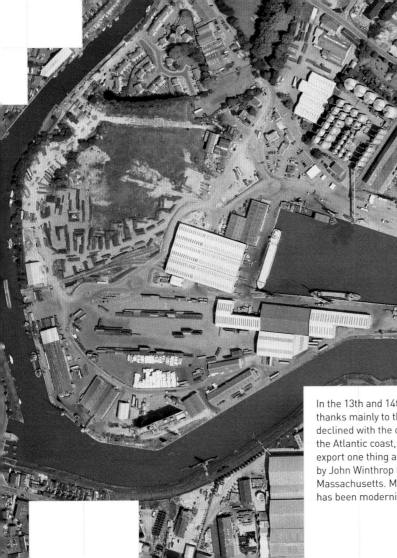

Boston
Lincolnshire

1. Seaport
2. United Nations carrier code: GB BOS
3. Vessel capacity: 5.5 m draught, 95 m length, 3,200 dwt
4. Goods handled: Containers, ro-ro, dry bulk (1.25m t/year)
5. Origin of name: Disputed – "Botwulf's stone" (referring to a boundary marker stone) or "Botolph's town"

England Photographic Atlas:
Page 368, A2

Authority: Port of Boston Ltd
Tel: (01205) 365571

In the 13th and 14th centuries Boston was England's second biggest seaport, thanks mainly to the flourishing wool trade with Flanders. Boston's fortunes declined with the opening up of the New World and the consequent shift of trade to the Atlantic coast, exacerbated by the silting up of the River Witham. Boston did export one thing across the Atlantic, though – its name. A group of emigrants led by John Winthrop left England via Southampton in 1630 and founded Boston, Massachusetts. More recently, with the shift of trade back towards Europe, the port has been modernized to handle goods passing to and from the European Union.

Brancaster Staithe
Norfolk

1. Resort & fishing port
2. Visitor numbers: Not recorded
3. Features: Boat trips to Scolt Head Island bird sanctuary
4. Industries: Tourism, sailing, fishing

England Photographic Atlas: Page 370, B2

Brancaster Staithe is renowned for its mussels and oysters, and its picturesque harbour is used both by fishermen and sailors. Boats depart from here for nearby Scolt Head Island, the most northerly point on the Norfolk coast and part of the North Norfolk Coast Site of Special Scientific Interest.

Cambridge Airport (Teversham)
2m e of Cambridge, Cambridgeshire

1. Opened: 8th October 1938
2. Air transport movements (2000): 1,643
3. Passengers (2000): 20,094
4. Runways: 05/23 (1,965 m) and 3 grass runways
5. Radio frequencies (MHz): 122.2 (tower)/ 123.6 (approach)

England Photographic Atlas: Page 324, D3

Operated by: Marshall Aerospace Ltd
Tel: (01223) 373737

Teversham is owned by Marshall Aerospace who, since its inception, have used the airport for the assembly, conversion, testing, and maintenance of aircraft – facilities include a temperature-controlled hangar for painting. The airport is also the home of the Cambridge University Air Squadron and the Cambridge Aero Club.

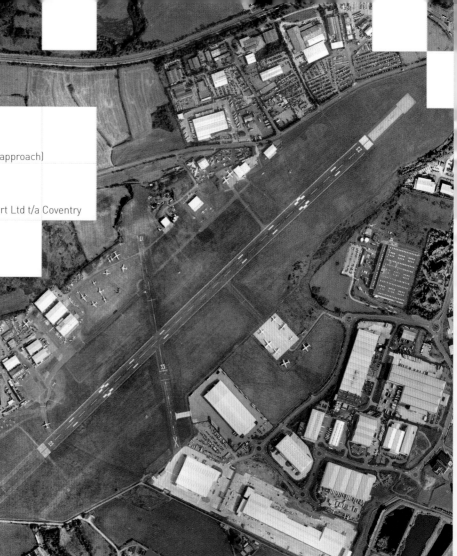

Coventry Airport (Baginton)
3m s of Coventry, West Midlands

1. Opened: 1937
2. Air transport movements (2000): 5,804
3. Passengers (2000): 3,993
4. Runways: 05/23 (1,615 m) & 17/35 (815 m)
5. Radio frequencies (MHz): 124.8 (tower)/119.25 (approach)

England Photographic Atlas: Page 419, G1

Operated by: West Midlands International Airport Ltd t/a Coventry Airport (a subsidiary of Atlantic Holdings Ltd)
Tel: (02476) 301717

Coventry Airport was opened as a municipal airport by the city council in conjunction with the aircraft manufacturer Armstrong Whitworth, which opened a factory on the site to produce bombers for the RAF. When the aircraft factory closed in 1965, civilian flights continued, with services to the Channel Islands, the Isle of Man and an aerial car ferry service to Calais. Various services and operators came and went before Air Atlantique moved to Baginton from Stansted in 1986, taking over operation of the airport from the city council as Atlantic Holdings in 1997. Air transport movements outnumber passengers at Baginton due to the high proportion of cargo flights.

East Midlands Airport (Castle Donington)

Castle Donington, East Midlands

1. Opened: RAF 1943, Civil 1965
2. Air transport movements (2000): 43,542
3. Passengers (2000): 2,234,494
4. Runway: 09/27 (2,280 m)
5. Radio frequencies (MHz): 124.00 (tower)/119.65 (approach)

England Photographic Atlas: Page 499, F4

Operated by: East Midlands International Airport Ltd
Tel: (01332) 852852

Castle Donington started life as a military airfield, opening in 1943 as a training base and closing down again just three and a half years later. It re-opened as a civilian airport in 1965 but, after nearly twenty years unused, it had to be almost entirely rebuilt, making it the first municipal airport to be built in Britain since the war. Since then it has grown rapidly as a cargo and passenger airport, with one of the first express parcel links in the 1980s, the arrival of United Parcels in the 1990s, and an £8m passenger terminal extension in 1996–97.

Harwich

Essex

1. Seaport
2. United Nations carrier code: GB HRW
3. Vessel capacity: 9.5 m draught, 480 m length
4. Goods handled: Ferry passengers, containers, ro-ro, general cargo, grain, dry bulk, oil, liquids, vehicles
5. Origin of name: Old English "army camp"

England Photographic Atlas: Page 314, D6

Authority: Harwich
International Port Ltd
Tel: (01255) 242000

The modern port of Harwich began as a rail ferry port built in the 1880s by the Great Eastern Railway (GER): in 1882, when the existing port became too small for the volume of traffic to the Low Countries, the GER built large new berths and a station two miles to the west, named Parkeston Quay after the company's chairman, Charles Parkes. The various reorganizations of the railways eventually saw Parkeston Quay become part of Sealink, which was privatized in 1984. Hutchison Port Holdings now has a 90% interest in Harwich International Port and has helped to develop a port already renowned for its freight and passenger ferry services into an efficient multipurpose port, the latest addition being a £1m grain terminal which opened in 1999.

Felixstowe
Suffolk

1. Port & resort
2. United Nations carrier code: GB FXT
3. Vessel capacity: 15 m draught, 630 m length
4. Goods handled: Containers, ro-ro, ferry passengers (freight c. 30 m t/year)
5. Origin of name: Old English "Filica's meeting place"

England Photographic Atlas: Page 315, D6

Authority: The Port of Felixstowe
Tel: (01394) 604500

Felixstowe became a fashionable holiday resort after a visit by the German Empress Augusta and her children in 1891. The industrial skyline of the modern port, now the UK's largest container port handling 41% of the country's container traffic, is at odds with the floral gardens, seafront promenade and the atmospheric Dooley Inn, whose many doors were used to facilitate the escape of the pub's patrons from Revenue men and Navy press gangs. The Port of Felixstowe comprises two container terminals with a combined total of 2,523 metres of quay as well as four ro-ro berths, one oil jetty and three general cargo berths.

Lakenheath Airfield
8m w of Thetford, Suffolk

1. Opened: 1941
2. Service: USAF
3. ICAO code: EGUL
4. Runway: 06/24 (2,743 m)
5. Squadrons: USAF 48th Fighter Wing (3 sqns)

England Photographic Atlas: Page 335, G2

Tel: (01638) 521861

Lakenheath opened under the wartime control of Bomber Command and was transferred to the US Air Force in 1948. Operations from this airfield during the Cold War included CIA-controlled reconnaissance flights using the U-2A, while more recent missions include the bombing of Libya in 1986 and Iraq in 1991.

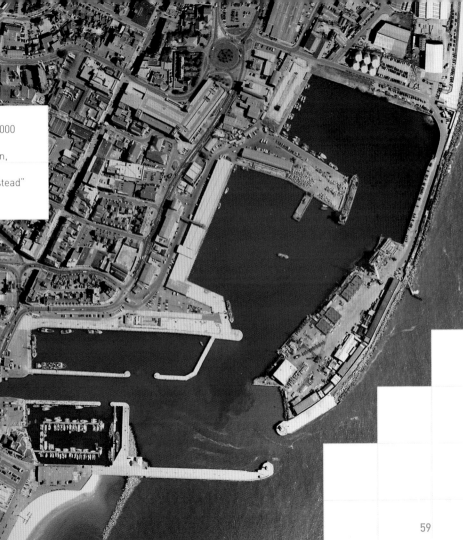

Lowestoft
Suffolk

1. Resort & fishing port
2. United Nations carrier code: GB LOW
3. Vessel capacity: 6 m draught, 125 m length, 6,000 dwt
4. Goods handled: Cement, containers, fish, grain, general cargo, offshore suplies, steel, timber
5. Origin of name: Old Danish "Hlothver's homestead"

England Photographic Atlas: Page 357, G6

Authority: Associated British Ports
Tel: (01502) 572286

Lowestoft Ness, just to the north of the harbour, is Britain's most easterly point, and Lowestoft itself is Britain's most easterly port. Britain's ports expanded hand in hand with the railways, and Lowestoft is no exception – initially run by the Lowestoft Railway & Harbour Company, the port was bought by the Eastern Counties Railway in 1848, which hugely improved port facilities over the following decade. With the nationalization of the railways in 1948, the port of Lowestoft came under the control of the British Transport Commission, later the British Transport Docks Board, and was finally privatized as part of Associated British Ports in 1983.

Luton Airport
Luton, Bedfordshire

1. Officially opened: 16th July 1938
2. Air transport movements (2000): 59,951
3. Passengers (2000): 6,190,499
4. Runway: 08/26 (2,160 m)
5. Radio frequencies (MHz): 132.55 (tower)/
   129.55, 128.75 (approach)

England Photographic Atlas: Page 293, E4

Operated by:
London Luton Airport Ltd
Tel: (01582) 395000

Luton Airport opened as a grass airfield
and developed slowly at first. It was 1959
before a hard runway was built, 1966
before the wooden terminal building was replaced by a new £1m
complex, and it took until 1978 before a government White
Paper officially recognised Luton as a fully-fledged international
airport. This sparked a major redevelopment that took five years
to complete and was officially opened by the Prince of Wales in
July 1985 – at last the modern Luton Airport was in operation,
and it is currently undergoing further expansion.

Mildenhall Airfield
12m n-w of Bury St Edmunds, Suffolk

1. Opened: 1934
2. Service: USAF/US Navy
3. ICAO code: EGUN
4. Runway: 11/29 (2,816 m)

England Photographic Atlas: Page 335, G2

Tel: (01638) 512251

Like its near-neighbour Lakenheath, Mildenhall spent the war under the control of Bomber Command. In 1950 control of the airfield was transferred to US Air Force, which used Mildenhall for various purposes including strategic reconnaissance using the Lockheed SR-71A "Blackbird", a plane capable of flying at speeds of more than 2,000 mph and at altitudes greater than 25,000 m.

Stansted Airport
3m n-e of Bishop's Stortford, Essex

1. Opened: USAAF 1943, Civil 1946
2. Air transport movements (2000): 146,660
3. Passengers (2000): 11,879,693
4. Runway: 05/23 (3,048 m)
5. Radio frequencies (MHz): 123.8, 125.55
   (tower)/120.625 (approach)

England Photographic Atlas: Page 297, F3

Operated by: British Airports Authority
Tel: (01279) 680500

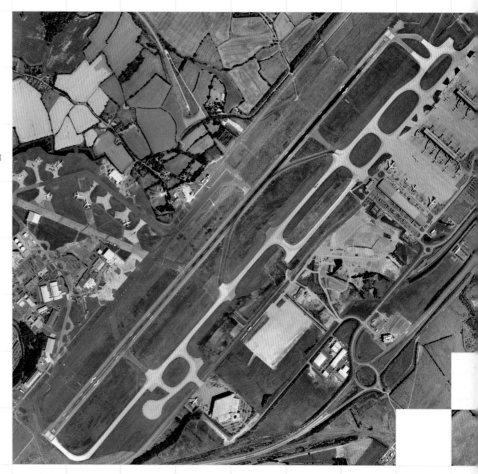

Stansted was built by the American forces
during the Second World War. Although
civilian operations began as early as 1946,
the Americans continued to develop the
airport through the 1950s during the Cold
War, including the provision of a 3,000 m
runway. The 1960s saw Stansted develop as
a freight centre, and a new cargo terminal
was completed in 1980; passenger traffic
also increased, and Stansted's future as
London's third airport was confirmed when
development work began in 1986. A
satellite passenger terminal was added in
1994 and plans are under way for further
extension of both passenger and freight
facilities.

the north

Barrow-in-Furness
Cumbria

1. Port
2. United Nations carrier code: GB BIF
3. Vessel capacity: 10 m draught, 230 m length, 15,000 dwt
4. Goods handled: Cruise passengers, gas condensate, limestone, nuclear fuels (cargo c. 0.25 m t/year)
5. Origin of name: Celtic and Old Norse "headland of the rump-shaped promontory"

England Photographic Atlas:
Page 670, C3

Authority: Associated British Ports
Tel: (01229) 822911

The industrial port of Barrow was created almost from scratch by the Furness Railway, which also became the port authority. In 1856 the railway company began to effect its plans, which included the enclosure of the Barrow Channel to form the Devonshire Dock (opened in 1867) and the Buccleuch Dock (1873). Ramsden Dock (1881) was used by both the Furness and the Midland Railways for steamers to and from Ireland until the Midland transferred its services to Heysham. Barrow is currently operated by Associated British Ports, and includes the country's largest shipyard, run by BAe Marine Services Ltd, used for the construction of surface vessels and nuclear submarines. Barrow is also a popular port of call for cruise liners because of its position as a gateway to the Lake District.

Berwick-upon-Tweed
Northumberland

1. Fishing port
2. United Nations carrier code: GB BWK
3. Vessel capacity: 4.6 m draught, 116 m length, 3,500 dwt
4. Goods handled: Fertiliser, grain, feed, forest products, general cargo, cement, stone (c. 0.15 m t/year)
5. Origin of name: Old English "barley farmstead" on the River Tweed (Tweed from Celtic "strong one")

England Photographic Atlas:
Page 746, D3

Authority: Berwick Harbour
Commission
Tel: (01289) 307404

At one time a prosperous Scottish port, Berwick-upon-Tweed changed hands thirteen times between 1174 and 1482 before finally becoming part of England. The town was heavily re-fortified during the reign of Elizabeth I to defend itself against a renewed French-Scottish alliance – the walls remain in a good state of repair because the French never attacked and Scotland was eventually united with England. Berwick boasts three bridges across the Tweed: the Berwick Bridge, a 15-arch stone bridge built in 1611 by order of James I, the concrete Royal Tweed Bridge (1928), and the Royal Border Railway Bridge, designed by Robert Stephenson in the 1840s.

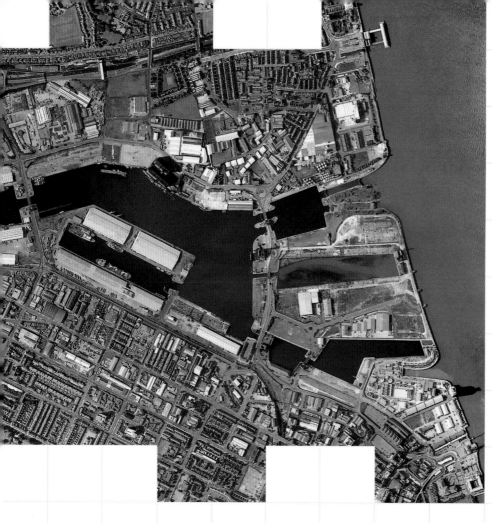

Birkenhead
Merseyside

1. Seaport
2. United Nations carrier code: GB LIV
3. Vessel capacity: 10 m draught
4. Goods handled: Dry bulk, forest products, foodstuffs, chemicals, petroleum products (33 m t/year Liverpool & Birkenhead combined)
5. Origin of name: Old English "headland overgrown with birch"

England Photographic Atlas: Page 557, F6

Authority: Mersey Docks & Harbour Company
Tel: (0151) 949 6000

Birkenhead, linked to Liverpool by the Mersey Tunnel (rail, 1886) and the Queensway Tunnel (road, 1934), has recently seen a £25m investment by the Mersey Dock & Harbour Company in the new Twelve Quays River Terminal. The terminal will be used by the ro-ro vessels of NorseMerchant Ferries and, being situated in the river rather than the enclosed docks, will reduce journey times to and from Ireland by 90 minutes.

Blyth
Northumberland

1. Port
2. United Nations carrier code: GB BLY
3. Vessel capacity: 8.5 m draught, 155 m length
4. Goods handled: Alumina, forest products, ammonium nitrate, coal, grain, stone, vehicles, containers (c. 1 m t/year)
5. Origin of name: Old English "the pleasant or cheerful one" (as in "blithe"), taken from the river on which it stands

England Photographic Atlas: Page 737, G4

Authority: Blyth Harbour Commission
Tel: (01670) 352066

The fishing town of Blyth made its name as a coal-exporting port after the Blyth & Tyne Railway reached the coast in the 1850s. The port (not under railway control) was redeveloped in 1880, prompting a resurgence in trade that lasted until the 1960s, the weight of coal handled increasing from a quarter of a million tons in 1880 to over 6 million by 1960. Freight has since declined, but Blyth is now famous as a pioneer of offshore wind resources – the rusting lighthouse shares the mile-long harbour wall with nine wind turbines, commissioned in 1993 by Border Wind Ltd and funded by the European Commission. The South Harbour is used by leisure craft, including the Royal Northumberland Yacht Club.

67

Goole
East Riding of Yorkshire

1. Inland seaport
2. United Nations carrier code: GB GOO
3. Vessel capacity: 4,500 dwt
4. Goods handled: Animal feed, containers, fertilisers, grain, iron, minerals, scrap metal, solid fuel, steel, timber (2.5 m t/year)
5. Origin of name: Middle English (place near the) "channel", "ditch" or "sluice"

England Photographic Atlas:
Page 649, F4

Authority: Associated British Ports
Tel: (01405) 766029

Goole is a seaport 42 miles from the sea, and it owes its existence as much to the canals and the railways as to the sea. The port grew rapidly following the cutting of a canal from Knottingley in 1826 as part of the Aire & Calder Navigation, and benefitted from massive investment by the Lancashire & Yorkshire Railway (LYR) in the late-19th and early-20th centuries. The LYR ran passenger and cargo services from Goole to the continent using a fleet of 30 ships, the greatest number owned by any of the railway companies. Associated British Ports has invested heavily in Goole since the docks were privatized in 1983, with the result that traffic levels are at their highest for 40 years.

Grimsby
Lincolnshire

1. Fishing port
2. United Nations carrier code: GB GSY
3. Vessel capacity: 5.8 m draught, 145 m length, 7,000 dwt
4. Goods handled: Vehicles, dry bulks, fish, general cargo, ro-ro freight, steel, timber
5. Origin of name: Old Danish "Grim's farmstead" (or village)

England Photographic Atlas:
Page 614, B1

Authority: Associated
British Ports
Tel: (01472) 359181

The early 14th century romance "The Lay of Havelok the Dane" tells of a fisherman named Grim who saves Havelok, the young prince of Denmark, by escaping with him to England and landing here, at the place that took Grim's name. Like many industrial ports, the develop-ment of modern Grimsby is tied in with the expansion of the railways: the Manchester Sheffield & Lincolnshire Railway bought the docks from the run-down Grimsby Dock Company, set up its own rail-ferry services to the Continent, built a fish dock, and in just ten years (1852-62) made Grimsby the country's fifth largest port in terms of value of trade. By 1912, the docks could expand no further, so the railway company, now the Great Central Railway, opened another dock at Immingham, six miles to the north-west (p. 74). At its peak, Grimsby had a trawler fleet of 260 ships, but fishing declined during the 1970s, when Icelandic waters closed to British fishing fleets after the Cod Wars.

Hartlepool
Cleveland

1. Port
2. United Nations carrier code: GB HTP
3. Vessel capacity: Length 190 m
4. Goods handled: Vehicles, fresh fruit, forest products, gypsum, steel, sand, limestone, grain, scrap
5. Origin of name: Old English (place by the) "stag (hart) peninsula bay"

England Photographic Atlas: Page 711, H5

Authority: Tees & Hartlepool Port Authority Ltd
Tel: (01429) 427405

Hartlepool developed under the lordship of the Bruce family, which had to relinquish its lands in England when Robert Bruce became king of Scotland – the town then became a prized target in the Anglo-Scottish Wars. The port had a revival during the 19th century, prompted by new docks built from 1835–41 by the Hartlepool Dock & Railway Company (HDRC). The need for expansion led to the opening of another new dock in 1852 by the Hartlepool West Harbour & Dock Company (HWHDC), and the consequent development of the new town of West Hartlepool. The HDRC became part of the North Eastern Railway in 1854 but railway politics kept the two docks separate until 1865, when the HWHDC also became part of the NER. The towns themselves remained separate entities until 1967 when they were united as Hartlepool.

Heysham
Lancashire

1. Seaside resort/ferry port
2. United Nations carrier code: GB HYM
3. Vessel capacity: 4.5 m draught, 167 m length, 16,640 dwt
4. Goods handled: Containers, ro-ro, ferry passengers
5. Origin of name: Old English "brushwood settlement"

England Photographic Atlas:
Page 658, B3

Authority: Heysham Port Ltd
Tel: (01524) 852373

The identities of the ancient villages of Heysham and Morecambe became blurred during the 20th century as they merged in the public perception into a single, extremely popular, holiday resort. At one time, the Midland Railway used a tidal pier at Morecambe for its ferry services to Belfast, but when this proved inadequate the railway company built a new dock at Heysham, which opened in 1904.

71

Humberside (Kingston upon Hull)
East Riding of Yorkshire

1. City & port
2. United Nations carrier code: GB HUL
3. Vessel capacity: 34,000 dwt
4. Goods handled: Ro-ro freight, ferry passengers (c. 1 m/year), steel, containers, dry and liquid bulks, forest products, general cargo, fish
5. Origin of name: Stands on the River Hull (Hull from Celtic "muddy"), Kingston added by Edward I (13th century)/Humberside from River Humber

England Photographic Atlas: Page 656, D1

Authority: Associated British Ports
Tel: (01482) 327171

Recorded in 1299 as Kyngeston super Hul, the city takes its royal title from Edward I, who laid out the seaport that was later to become Britain's third largest after London and Liverpool. The original docks have now become city-centre public gardens (Queen's Gardens), shopping centres (Prince's Quay) and marinas, while the modern industrial docks, seen here, have spread inexorably eastwards along the Humber Estuary. Famous sons and daughters, adopted and otherwise, include anti-slavery campaigner William Wilberforce, aviatrix Amy Johnson, Deputy Prime Minister John Prescott, and poet Philip Larkin.

Immingham
Lincolnshire

1. Bulk cargo port
2. United Nations carrier code: GB IMM
3. Vessel capacity: 10.3 m draught, 198 m length, 38,000 dwt (dock)/300,000 dwt (riverside terminals)
4. Goods handled: Animal feed, coal, dry bulks, general cargo, forest products, grain, iron ore, liquid petroleum, petrochemicals, ro-ro freight, steel (c. 45 m t/year)
5. Origin of name: Old English "homestead of Imma's people"

England Photographic Atlas: Page 651, H5

Authority: Associated British Ports
Tel: (01469) 571555

The history of Immingham is firmly entwined with that of Grimsby (p. 68), further south and east on the Humber Estuary. When the Great Central Railway ran out of space to expand the port of Grimsby in 1912, the company built a new port at Immingham, capable of handling the largest cargo vessels built at the time and still one of Britain's largest ports. As part of Associated British Ports (ABP), Grimsby and Immingham remain linked, together making up one of ABP's five business units.

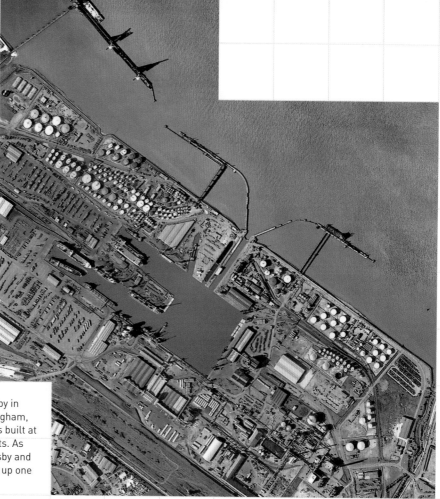

Leeds-Bradford International Airport (Yeadon)
Between Leeds and Bradford, West Yorkshire

1. Opened: 1931
2. Air transport movements (2000): 29,263
3. Passengers (2000): 1,585,039
4. Runways: 14/32 (2,250 m) & 10/28 (1,100 m)
5. Radio frequencies (MHz): 120.3 (tower)/123.75 (approach)

England Photographic Atlas: Page 662, C6

Operated by: Leeds-Bradford Airport Ltd
Tel: (0113) 250 9696

Scheduled passenger flights did not begin at Yeadon until four years after the airport opened, and were suspended four years after that for the duration of the Second World War. For most of the war, Yeadon was used by Avro for aircraft production and testing, and was afterwards returned to the Ministry of Civil Aviation. A new runway was added in 1965, a new terminal in 1968, and a 600 m runway extension in 1982 allowed 747s and Tri-Stars to use the airport. Restricted opening hours stifled the airport's further growth until 24-hour opening was introduced in 1993, leading to a massive increase in traffic and the consequent expansion of the airport itself.

Liverpool Docks (north)
Merseyside

1. City & seaport
2. United Nations carrier code: GB LIV
3. Vessel capacity: 22 m draught,
   346 m length, 322,912 dwt
4. Goods handled: Petroleum products,
   crude oil, containers, ro-ro, general cargo, cruise
   passengers, dry bulk, chemicals (33 m t/year
   Liverpool & Birkenhead combined)
5. Origin of name: Old English "muddy creek (or pool)",
   referring to the tidal creek around which the
   settlement was founded

England Photographic Atlas: Page 557,

Authority: Mersey Docks & Harbour Company
Tel: (0151) 949 6000

Liverpool grew to be "the Empire's second city" on the
back of the slave trade, which prompted the building of
the first dock in 1715 – there are now more than seven
miles of docks, although their use has declined
dramatically. After abolition, the city continued to
handle people as well as freight, with nine million
emigrants leaving Europe via Liverpool for America and
the southern hemisphere between 1830 and 1930. Trade
has dwindled since and this is reflected in the fact that
other uses are being found for many of the docks – the
former Albert Dock is now the home of Tate Liverpool.

Liverpool Airport (Speke)
6m s-e of Liverpool

1. Opened: 1930 (licensed 1933)
2. Air transport movements (2000): 32,442
3. Passengers (2000): 1,982,711
4. Runway: 09/27 (2,286 m)
5. Radio frequencies (MHz): 118.1 (tower)/
   119.85 (approach)

England Photographic Atlas: Page 553, G5

Operated by: Liverpool Airport plc
Tel: (0151) 288 4000

By the outbreak of the Second World War, Speke had become one of the UK's busiest airports, and it was one of the few to continue civilian flights during the war. The present runway was built in 1961 (one of the original runways was extended at the same time), and in 1979 the airport was chosen as the centre of the Post Office mail flight organization, which now has a dedicated building for the mail interchange. The original airfield closed in 1982 and a new control tower, apron and passenger building were built from 1982–85, closer to what had now become the airport's only runway

Manchester Airport (Ringway)
10m s of Manchester

1. Opened: 25th June 1938
2. Air transport movements (2000): 178,468
3. Passengers (2000): 18,568,709
4. Runways: 06L/24R (3,048 m) & 06R/24L (3,048 m)
5. Radio frequencies (MHz): 118.625 (tower)/119.4, 118.575 (approach)

England Photographic Atlas: Page 577, F3

Operated by: Manchester Airport plc
Tel: (0161) 489 3000

Ringway opened in 1938 and was almost immediately commandeered for wartime use as a parachute training school, before civilian flights restarted in 1946. The airport underwent a huge reconstruction programme from 1957–62 and was redeveloped again in the 1970s to accommodate the new wide-bodied airliners, making Ringway the UK's largest airport outside London. A new domestic terminal opened in 1989 and the controversial second runway, seen to the south of the original, opened on 5th February 2001 at a cost of £172m.

Newcastle Airport (Woolsington)
6m n-w of Newcastle, Tyne & Wear

1. Opened: 1935
2. Air transport movements (2000): 43,846
3. Passengers (2000): 3,208,734
4. Runway: 07/25 (2,332 m)
5. Radio frequencies (MHz): 119.7
   (tower)/124.375 (approach)

England Photographic Atlas: Page 712, C1

Operated by:
Newcastle
International
Airport Ltd
Tel: (0191) 286 0966

Woolsington opened with services to Edinburgh and London, and four years later was requisitioned by the Air Ministry for the duration of the Second World War. A new runway was built in 1955 and the terminal buildings expanded in 1966–67. Further expansion and improvements took place almost continuously from 1981 until the mid-1990s to cope with the growing volume of traffic using the airport.

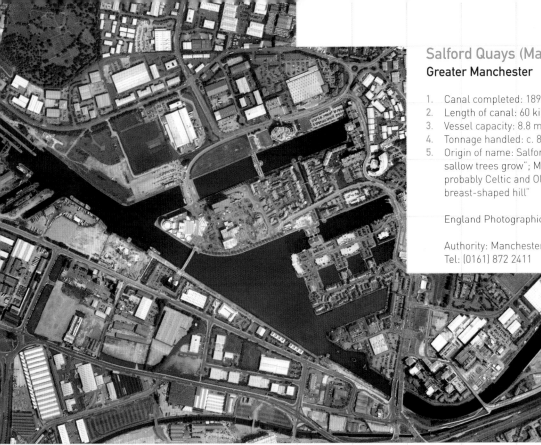

Salford Quays (Manchester Ship Canal)
Greater Manchester

1. Canal completed: 1894
2. Length of canal: 60 kilometres
3. Vessel capacity: 8.8 m daught, 246 m length
4. Tonnage handled: c. 8.5 m/year
5. Origin of name: Salford – Old English "ford where sallow trees grow"; Manchester – uncertain, probably Celtic and Old English "Roman fort on the breast-shaped hill"

England Photographic Atlas: Page 585, E5

Authority: Manchester Ship Canal Company
Tel: (0161) 872 2411

Salford Quays were built to serve the Manchester Ship Canal, which in turn was built to attract trade to Manchester from Liverpool. There are several wharves at Salford Quays, including the private wharf of Cerestar Ltd at Trafford Park, which discharges grain to large silos at the company's Trafford Park plant. The Irwell Park Wharf handles dry bulk, and there is also an oil terminal, serving oil-processing plants at Barton and Mode Wheel.

Scarborough
North Yorkshire

1. Fishing port, resort & spa town
2. United Nations carrier code: GB SCA
3. Vessel capacity: 4.6 m draught, 79.8 m length, 2,410 dwt
4. Goods handled: Fishing boats and pleasure craft (no cargo vessels since 1994)
5. Origin of name: Old Norse and Old English "Skarthi's stronghold"

England Photographic Atlas: Page 682, C3

Authority: Scarborough Borough Council
Tel: (01723) 373530

Scarborough, founded by a Viking rejoicing in the name of Scarthi or Scardi, meaning harelip, is the country's oldest seaside resort. The town's first visitors arrived in the early 17th century and they were drawn not by the sea and the sand but by Scarborough's mineral springs. Soon visitors to the spa also began venturing onto the beach and into the sea, pioneering the hitherto unheard-of idea of "sea-bathing", and by the 19th century Scarborough was known as "the Queen of the Watering Places". The town has also long been a fishing port, its harbour busy with cobles and mules (traditional fishing boats), drifters and trawlers.

Seahouses
Northumberland

1. Fishing village & resort
2. Visitor numbers: Not reported
3. Features: Boat trips to the Farne Islands
4. Industries: Fishing, tourism
5. Origin of name: "Houses by the sea"

England Photographic Atlas: Page 745, G2

Tourist office tel: (01665) 720884

The population of the Nothumberland fishing village of Seahouses swells on summer week-ends with tourists visiting the village to enjoy the sandy beaches and National Trust dunes to the north, or to depart by boat for the Farne Islands nature reserve just off the coast. To the east of the village is the Seafield Caravan Park.

Sheffield City Airport
4m n-e of Sheffield, South Yorkshire

1. Officially opened: 10th June 1997
2. Air transport movements (2000): 4,247
3. Passengers (2000): 60,636
4. Runway: 10/28 (1,199 m)
5. Radio frequency (MHz): 128.525 (tower and approach)

England Photographic Atlas: Page 602, A5

Operated by: Sheffield City Airport Ltd
Tel: (0114) 201 1998

Sheffield City Council first discussed the idea of a municipal airport in 1919 but by the time sites were surveyed in 1931, an airport was considered too expensive, and for the next 60 years Sheffield was the largest city in Europe not to have its own airport. Plans for an airport were revived in 1988 but it was still nine years before it officially opened, and another eight months before the first scheduled flights began with a thrice daily service to Amsterdam.

Staithes
North
Yorkshire

1. Fishing village
2. Visitor numbers: Not reported
3. Features: Cowbar Nab, a sheer cliff-face to the north
4. Industries: Fishing, tourism
5. Origin of name: Old Norse "landing stage or wharf"

England Photographic Atlas: Page 701, E3

The cottages at Staithes seem to cling to the steep cliff-face in an attempt to shelter from the harsh weather of this part of the coast. James Cook worked for a short time in a haberdasher's shop in Staithes (the shop succumbed to the weather in 1745) before being apprenticed to a Whitby ship-owner (p. 90) and embarking on his career as an explorer.

Sunderland
Tyne & Wear

1. City & port
2. United Nations carrier code: GB SUN
3. Vessel capacity: 10.4 m draught, 200 m length, 52,000 dwt
4. Goods handled: Dry & liquid bulks, forest products, steel products, metals, machinery (c. 1.2 m t/year)
5. Origin of name: Disputed – "detached land" (ie separated from the estate to which it belonged), or "divided land" (divided by the river)

England Photographic Atlas: Page 717, F3

Authority: Port of Sunderland
Tel: (0191) 553 2100

The Port of Sunderland dates back more than 800 years, the earliest evidence of maritime commerce being a charter granted in 1154. Sunderland grew in importance, first as a coal-exporting port, and then as a ship-building centre, until by 1840 there were 65 shipyards on the river, and Sunderland took its place as the world's biggest shipbuilding port. Sadly, less than 150 years later, in 1988, Sunderland witnessed the closure of its last shipyard.

Teesside
Teesside

1. Estuary and harbour mouth
2. United Nations carrier code: GB TEE
3. Ports: Tees ports include Middlesbrough, Billingham and Redcar
4. Industries: High technology, plastics, petrochemicals, electronics, chemicals, oil, gas
5. Origin of name: From the River Tees, Celtic "boiling, surging one"

England Photographic Atlas:
Page 700, A1

Authority: Tees & Hartlepool Port Authority Ltd
Tel: (01642) 877000

The industrial areas close to the mouth of the River Tees include Teesport (bottom centre of the picture), the tidal Seal Sands (top left), North Sea oil and gas terminals (south and east of Seal Sands) and a number of chemical and petro-chemical works. Further upstream are the Tees ports of Billingham on the north bank and Middlesbrough on the south.

Tyneside
Tyne & Wear

1. Industrial towns & ports
2. United Nations carrier code: GB TYN
3. Ports: Newcastle, North & South Shields, Jarrow, Tynemouth, Wallsend and Gateshead
4. Industries: Electrical goods, cables, chemicals, paint, fishing, tourism
5. Origin of name: Tyne, "the river"; North and South Shields, "temporary sheds or huts" (for offshore fishing); Jarrow, "settlement of the fen people"; Wallsend stands at the end of Hadrian's wall; Gateshead, "goat's headland or hill"

England Photographic Atlas: Page 727, F5

Authority: Port of Tyne Authority
Tel: (0191) 455 2671

When the railways were nationalized in 1948 many of the former railway ports came under the control of British Transport Commission and later the British Transport Docks Board (BTDB). During the 1960s a government committee recommended that BTDB ports should be grouped together by estuary, which led to the formation of the Port of Tyne comprising the towns along the river estuary. Newcastle has been the focus of the area since the Romans bridged the Tyne here, and the city maintained its prominence as an Elizabethan coal port (hence the well-known phrase) and then as a ship-building centre. Traditional industries have declined, with only 1% of Newcastle's workforce now in heavy industry and over 80% in the public or service sectors.

Whitby
North Yorkshire

1. Port & resort
2. United Nations carrier code: GB WTB
3. Vessel capacity: 5 m draught, 85 m length, 3,000 dwt
4. Goods handled: Steel, malt, fishing boats
5. Origin of name: Old Scandinavian "Hviti's village"

England Photographic Atlas:
Page 701, H4

Authority: Scarborough Borough Council
Harbour Master tel: (01947) 602354

Herring was Whitby's main catch for at least a thousand years until whaling took over in the 18th century, with such success that Herman Melville waxes lyrical about the town's whaling captains in his novel Moby Dick. Another literary connection is that Bram Stoker had the idea for Dracula while on holiday here in 1890. The ship carrying Dracula's coffin is wrecked on Tate Hill Sands (Stoker based his account on newspaper reports of a real shipwreck of the time) – Dracula then comes ashore and, in the form of a large dog, bounds up the 199 steps to St Mary's church, whose graveyard he uses as his base. Captain Cook, explorer of the Pacific and the Southern Ocean, was apprenticed to a Whitby ship-owner, and all four of Cook's famous ships were built here.

scotland

Aberdeen Airport (Dyce)

7m n-w of Aberdeen, Aberdeenshire

1. Opened: 1934
2. Air transport movements (2000): 82,550
3. Passengers (2000): 2,488,597
4. Runways: 16/34 (1,820 m), 05/23 & 14/32 used by helicopters
5. Radio frequencies (MHz): 118.1 (tower)/120.4 (approach)

   Operated by: British Airports Authority
   Tel: (01224) 722331

Dyce was a relatively quiet airport until the discovery of oil and gas in the North Sea led to a massive rise in helicopter traffic serving the offshore oil platforms, of which there are now over 100. From 1975–77 the airport was greatly expanded and, as well as providing scheduled flights to British and European destinations, it is now the world's busiest heliport.

92

Aberdeen
Aberdeenshire

1. City and port
2. United Nations carrier code: GB ABD
3. Vessel capacity: 10 m draught, 116 m length
4. Industries: North Sea oil, paper manufacturing, textiles, engineering, food processing, chemicals
5. Origin of name: Celtic-Pictish "mouth of the River Don" (modern Aberdeen stands on the River Dee but the name stems from Old Aberdeen, further north on the River Don)

Authority: Aberdeen
Harbour Board
Tel: (01224) 597000

Aberdeen has been an important fishing port since the 13th century. The Victoria Dock to the north, the Albert Basin and the River Dee to the south form Aberdeen's three-pronged harbour, with the P&O Shetland ferry sailing from Victoria dock, and the Albert basin used mainly for commercial traffic. Since the 1970s, the city's fortunes have revolved around North Sea oil and gas which has seen huge investment in the harbour, airport, schools, housing and offshore developments.

Arbroath
Angus

1. Fishing town
2. United Nations carrier code: GB ARB
3. Vessel capacity: 4.4 m draught, 70 m length
4. Goods handled: Fishing boats and leisure craft (no commercial cargo since 1997)
5. Origin of name: Celtic-Pictish "mouth of the Brothock Water" (Brothock from Scottish-Gaelic "boiling/turbulent")

Authority: Angus County Council
Tel: (01241) 872166

Arbroath, aka Aberbrothock, has been a fishing port since the 12th century, and the town's main catch of haddock has given rise to one of Scotland's favourite national dishes, the Arbroath Smokie. Arbroath is also famous for its 13th-century abbey (now ruined), which was the scene of the Declaration of Arbroath in 1320, asking the Pope to reverse his excommunication of Robert Bruce and to recognize Scotland's independence from England.

Ardrossan
North Ayrshire

1. Ferry port
2. United Nations carrier code: GB ARD
3. Vessel capacity: 7.78 m draught
4. Goods handled: Ferry passengers, containers, ro-ro
5. Origin of name: Scottish Gaelic "height of the little cape"

Authority: Ardrossan Harbour Company Ltd
Tel: (01294) 463972

Ardrossan was a small fishing village until 1805, when the 12th Earl of Eglinton began to develop a seaport which, by 1840, was busy exporting coal from the Eglinton family mines. Most of Ardrossan's industries have now declined but there is still a small oil refinery. The town is the main ferry port for Arran and also handles commercial traffic to Ireland.

Ayr
South Ayrshire

1. Resort & port
2. United Nations carrier code: GB AYR
3. Vessel capacity: 5.8 m draft, 95 m length
4. Goods handled: Dry bulk
5. Origin of name: Stands on the River Ayr (Ayr pre-Celtic, possibly "smooth-running")

Authority: Associated British Ports
Tel: (01292) 281687

Ayr grew up as an industrial port but by the early 18th century it was described by Daniel Defoe as being "like an old beauty, shewing the ruins of a good face... the reason for its decay is the decay of its trade... nothing will save it from death if trade does not revive". Industry did not revive to its former levels, but in the 19th century Ayr found a new role as a seaside resort, with a racecourse, three golf courses and miles of golden sands.

Clydebank (Renfrew)

Renfrewshire

1. Town and port
2. United Nations carrier code: GB GLW
3. Vessel capacity: 7.3 m draught, 757 m length (King George V dock)
4. Goods handled: Steel, timber, minerals, dry bulk, project cargo, general cargo, ro-ro
5. Origin of name: Clyde, Celtic "cleansing one"/Renfrew, Celtic "point of the torrent"

Authority: Clydeport Operations Ltd
Tel: (0141) 221 8733

The "torrent" that gives Renfrew its name was created by the confluence of the Black and White Cart rivers with the Clyde. By 1614, Renfrew was the principal Clyde port, and continued to expand during the 19th and early 20th centuries, with shipbuilding established in 1844 and steel manufacturing in 1907. Both of these industries have since declined.

Dundee

Dundee

1. City & fishing port
2. United Nations carrier code:
   GB DUN
3. Vessel capacity: 9 m draught
4. Industries: Fishing,
   engineering, textiles,
   electronics, printing, food
   processing
5. Origin of name: Disputed –
   "fort of Daig", "fort of Tay",
   "dark hill" or "hill of God"

Authority: Port of Dundee Ltd
Tel: (01382) 224121

Dundee stands on the Firth of Tay and is linked to the south side of the firth by two bridges, the 1.5 mile Tay Road Bridge, opened in 1966, and the 2 mile Tay Rail Bridge, opened in 1887 to replace the one that collapsed in 1879. The port of Dundee thrived on whaling in the 18th century, with the jute trade and ship-building taking over in the 19th – Shackleton's Terra Nova was Dundee-built, and Captain Scott's Discovery, built here in 1901, is now preserved in the remaining city docks. The Earl Grey Dock (1843) was filled to form the northern landfall of the Tay Road Bridge (seen here), while the Camperdown and Victoria Docks (1960s) survive to the east.

Edinburgh (Leith)
Edinburgh

1. Port
2. United Nations carrier code: GB LEI
3. Vessel capacity: 9.75 m draught, 210 m length
4. Goods handled: Wheat, maize, barley, coal, pipes (c2 m t/year)
5. Origin of name: Disputed – Celtic "moist" or Scottish Gaelic "grey"

Authority: Forth Ports plc
Tel: (0131) 554 4343

Leith was granted to the city of Edinburgh by Robert Bruce in 1329 to serve as the city's port, became an independent burgh in 1833, and was once again incorporated in Edinburgh in 1920. Mary Queen of Scots landed here when she returned to Scotland in 1561, having spent her childhood in France. The port became an important ship-building centre during the 17th century and Scotland's first dry docks were built here in 1720. Ship-building ended in 1984 after which Leith, somewhat surprisingly, found itself regenerated as a popular waterfront eating-place and is now considered to have some of the best pubs and restaurants in Edinburgh. The harbour is now the home of the former Royal Yacht Britannia.

Edinburgh Airport (Turnhouse)

8m w of Edinburgh

1. Opened: Military 1915, Civil 1947
2. Air transport movements (2000): 89,142
3. Passengers (2000): 5,523,559
4. Runways: 07/25 (2,560 m), 13/31 (1,796 m) & 08/26 (909 m)
5. Radio frequencies (MHz): 118.7 (tower)/121.2 (approach)

Operated by: British Airports Authority
Tel: (0131) 333 1000

Turnhouse was built as a First World War military airfield and spent the Second World War under the control of Fighter Command, before civil flights began in 1947. Like Aberdeen, Edinburgh reaped the benefits of increased traffic from the North Sea oil companies, and the airport was massively redeveloped from 1971–77, including the provision of a new runway and terminal building.

Glasgow Airport (Abbotsinch)
10m w of Glasgow

1. Opened: RAF 1932, Civil 1966
2. Air transport movements (2000): 90,607
3. Passengers (2000): 6,965,500
4. Runways: 05/23 (2,658 m) & 10/28 (1,104 m)
5. Radio frequencies (MHz): 118.8 (tower)/119.1 (approach)

Operated by: British Airports Authority
Tel: (0141) 887 1111

Abbotsinch was built for the RAF but transferred to the Fleet Air Arm in 1943. The airfield remained a Royal Naval Air Station until 1963, after which it was redeveloped as a civil airport. During the 1990s a £55 m expansion project took place which included a new car park, extensions to the terminal, and a new international pier.

Glasgow Prestwick International Airport
7m s of Kilmarnock, East Ayrshire

1. Opened: Scottish Aviation 1935, Civil post-WWII
2. Air transport movements (2000): 11,428
3. Passengers (2000): 910,023
4. Runways: 13/31 (2,987 m) & 03/21 (1,829 m)
5. Radio frequencies (MHz): 118.15 (tower)/120.55 (approach)

Operated by: Prestwick International Airport Ltd
Tel: (01292) 479822

Scottish Aviation's Monkton Airfield became an RAF station in 1939 and a civil airport immediately after the war, at which time it was Britain's second most important airport after Heathrow. Prestwick remained west Scotland's main international terminal until the 1990s, when many operators transferred their services to Glasgow following the expansion of Abbotsinch Airport (previous page). Improved rail links with Glasgow, and re-branding as Glasgow Prestwick International Airport, have seen something of a resurgence in Prestwick's fortunes.

Inverness
Highland

1. Tourist centre & port
2. United Nations carrier code: GB INV
3. Vessel capacity: 6.25 m draught, 120 m length
4. Goods handled: Timber, coal, salt, oil, grain, forest products (c. 0.75m t/year)
5. Origin of name: Scottish Gaelic "mouth of the River Ness" (Ness meaning "roaring" or "rushing")

Authority: Inverness Harbour Trust
Tel: (01463) 715715

Historically, Inverness came to prominence because of its strategic importance controlling routes both north-south and east-west across Scotland, being both at the head of Loch Ness (to which it is linked by the Caledonian Canal) and at the crossing of the Moray Firth – the present road bridge can be seen carrying the A9 across the Firth northwards out of the picture. The port traded with England and the Baltic, while a plentiful supply of timber allowed a ship-building industry to thrive. Inverness is currently important as the administrative centre for the Highland region, and the port remains busy trading with Scandinavia, the European Union and the Baltic.

Inverness Airport (Dalcross)
8m n-e of Inverness, Highland

1. Opened: RAF WWII, Civil 1947
2. Air transport movements (2000): 10,712
3. Passengers (2000): 360,698
4. Runways: 06/24 (1,887 m) & 12/30 (700 m)
5. Radio frequency (MHz): 122.6 (tower and approach)

Operated by: Highlands and Islands Airports Ltd
Tel: (01667) 464000

Dalcross was used for advanced flying training during the Second World War and again during the 1950s. Civil traffic increased hugely with the North Sea oil business and the airport was expanded in 1979 as a result.

Mallaig
Highland

1. Fishing and ferry port
2. United Nations carrier code: GB MLG
3. Vessel capacity: 6 m draught, 90 m length
4. Goods handled: Fish, ro-ro, ferry passengers
5. Origin of name: Disputed – Old Norse and Scottish Gaelic "headland bay", or Old Norse "shingle bay"

Authority: Mallaig Harbour Authority
Tel: (01687) 462154

Mallaig is the main ferry port for the Isle of Skye and, because of its position further south, has not suffered the same decline in ferry traffic as Kyle of Lochalsh since the opening of the Skye Bridge. The town is also the departure point for Rum, Eigg, Muck and Canna, and supports a fishing fleet that still thrives, having switched from herring to prawn fishing.

Montrose
Angus

1. Port
2. United Nations carrier code: GB MON
3. Vessel capacity: 7.6 m draught, 164 m length, 17,190 dwt
4. Goods handled: Wood pulp, paper, grain, roundwood, scrap steel (c. 0.75m t/year)
5. Origin of name: Scottish Gaelic "peat moss of the promontory"

Authority: Montrose Port Authority
Tel: (01674) 672302

Montrose has been a seaport since the 13th century and is now a popular sailing centre. The town is famous for the Montrose Basin, a two-mile-square tidal basin to the west of the town, now home to the Montrose Basin Wildlife Centre. When the tide is in, Montrose is bounded on three sides by water, with the North Sea to the east, the Montrose Basin to the west and the South Esk River to the south.

Peterhead
Aberdeenshire

1. Industrial seaport
2. United Nations carrier code: GB PHD
3. Vessel capacity: 6 m draught, 170 m length
4. Goods handled: Coal, fish oil, fish, salt, fertilisers, animal feed, grain, rape seed, peat, fuel oil (c. 0.25 m t/year)
5. Origin of name: Scottish Gaelic "St Peter's headland"

Authority: Peterhead Harbour Trustees
Tel: (01779) 474281

Peterhead, founded in 1593 at the mouth of the River Ugie, is the most easterly town in Scotland and takes its name from St Peter's Kirk, which was built on the headland in 1132. One of Britain's biggest whaling ports during the 19th century, the harbour is now used by service industries for North Sea oil.

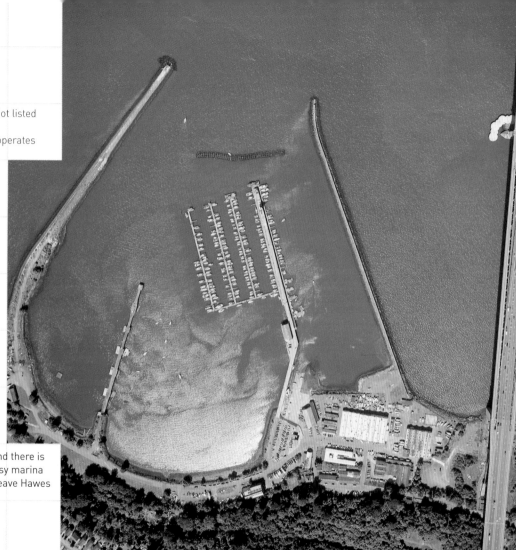

South Queensferry
Edinburgh

1. Town & marina
2. United Nations carrier code: Not listed
3. Vessel capacity: Not listed
4. Features: "Maid of the Forth" operates pleasure cruises on the Forth
5. Origin of name: Commemorates Queen Margaret, wife of 11th century King Malcolm

Authority: Forth Ports plc
Tel: (0131) 554 6473

During the 11th century, Queen Margaret, after whom Queensferry is named, used a ferry here to travel between Edinburgh and the royal residence at Dunfermline. A public ferry was established by King David I in 1129 and lasted more than 800 years before it was replaced in 1964 by the Forth Road Bridge, visible in this picture. During the 17th century, Queensferry was a busy trading port, and although trade has declined and there is no longer a ferry, there is a busy marina and pleasure boats regularly leave Hawes Pier for cruises on the Forth.

Stonehaven
Aberdeenshire

1. Fishing port
2. Visitors to tourist office: Not reported
3. Features: Boat trips to Fowlsheugh RSPB reserve
4. Industries: Tourism, fishing
5. Origin of name: Disputed – Old English "stony landing place" or Old Norse "stony harbour"

Tourist office tel: (01569) 762806

Although no shipbuilding or repairs take place in the fishing village of Stonehaven, the town has made a huge contribution to that industry, being the birthplace of Robert William Thomson, who invented a portable steam crane and a hydraulic dock (as well as a pneumatic tyre and an improved fountain pen).

Troon
South Ayrshire

1. Resort & port
2. United Nations carrier code: GB TRN
3. Vessel capacity: 6.2 m draught, 130 m length, 6,000 dwt
4. Goods handled: Logwood, minerals
5. Origin of name: Disputed – Celtic "headland" or Scottish Gaelic "nose" or "point"

Authority: Associated British Ports
Tel: (01292) 281687

Troon benefits from a natural harbour formed by the promontory from which the town takes its name. The port was developed during the early 19th century by the 4th Duke of Portland for shipping coal to Ireland, and the new town was laid out around the harbour. The port began to thrive with the opening of the Kilmarnock and Troon Railway in 1812, transporting coal from the former to the latter, and the Ailsa Shipbuilding Company, established shortly afterwards, is still in evidence in this photograph. Tourism grew alongside industry and Troon is now far more famous for its golf courses than for its port.

wales and northern ireland

Aberystwyth
Ceredigion

1. Resort
2. Visitors to tourist office: Not reported
3. Features: Castle (1211), National Library of Wales
4. Industries: Tourism, university town
5. Origin of name: Old Welsh "mouth of the Ystwyth"

Tourist office tel: (01970) 612125

Aberystwyth is actually a misnomer, because the modern town stands not on the River Ystwyth but on the River Rheidol – the town's name stems from an earlier 12th-century settlement which was indeed on the Ystwyth, slightly further to the south. The National Library is housed within the original buildings of the University of Wales which stand on Aberystwyth's promenade.

Barmouth (Abermaw)
Gwynedd

1. Resort
2. Visitors to tourist office: Not reported
3. Features: Ty Gwyn Museum, Ty Crwn Roundhouse
4. Industries: Tourism
5. Origin of name: Old Welsh "mouth of the River Mawddach" (Barmouth is an anglicised corruption of the Welsh Abermawddach and became the town's official title in 1768 – the modern Welsh name is often shortened to "Bermo")

Tourist office tel: (01341) 280787

Approaching Barmouth from the south, the railway crosses the estuary of the River Mawddach on a spectacular 750 m, 113-span wooden bridge. Attractions include the Dinas Oleu cliffs, which in 1895 became the first property to be acquired by the National Trust.

Barry (Barri)
Vale of Glamorgan

1. Port & resort
2. United Nations carrier code: GB BAD
3. Vessel capacity: 9 m draught, 175 m length, 27,343 dwt
4. Goods handled: Chemicals, oil, fruit, cement clinker
5. Origin of name: Old Welsh "the hill place"

Authority: Associated British Ports
Tel: (02920) 400500

Barry grew at an enormous pace when it began exporting coal, from a village of 85 inhabitants in 1880 to a town with a population of almost 50,000 a century later. Together with Barry Island, which is connected to the mainland by a tidal causeway, Barry is now a major tourist resort with one of the largest amusement parks in Britain.

Belfast (Beal Feirste)
Belfast, County Antrim and County Down

1. City & industrial port
2. United Nations carrier code: GB BEL
3. Vessel capacity: 10.5 m draught
4. Goods handled: Containers, ro-ro, dry and liquid bulk, liquefied gas (c. 12.5 m t/year)
5. Origin of name: Irish Gaelic "sandbank at the mouth"

Authority: Belfast Harbour Commissioners
Tel: (01232) 554422

The odd-sounding derivation of the name Belfast reflects the importance of a ford made possible by the presence of a sandbank at the mouth of the River Farset where it joins the Lagan, the ford being the reason that Belfast grew up where it did. By the late 17th century, the town had grown into a busy port whose main industries were the manufacture of brick, rope, net and sailcloth, and by the start of the 18th century, Belfast had superseded Carrickfergus as the region's main port. Ship-building became firmly established during the 19th century and reached its peak with Harland and Wolff, builders of the Titanic, but the shipbuilding industry declined during the 20th century.

Belfast International Airport (Aldergrove)
County Antrim, 13m n-w of Belfast

1. Opened: Military 1918, Civil 1963
2. Air transport movements (2000): 43,010
3. Passengers (2000): 3,148,577
4. Runways: 07/25 (2,777 m) & 17/35 (1,951 m)
5. Radio frequencies (MHz): 118.3 (tower)/120.9 (approach)

Operated by: Belfast International Airport Ltd
Tel: (028) 9442 2888

Aldergrove came under the control of Coastal Command for the duration of the Second World War, having been used by the military since 1918. The airfield was rebuilt as a civil airport during the 1960s. It opened with all mod-cons when services were transferred on 26th September 1963 from the previous civil airfield at Nutts Corner, where there was no room for expansion. Huge investments were made during the 1990s, including an extension to the East Terminal and the building of a new cargo complex with its own separate terminal.

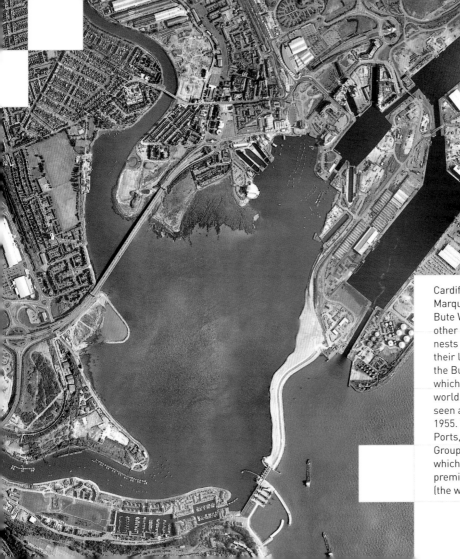

Cardiff (Caerdydd)

1. Seaport & capital of Wales
2. United Nations carrier code: GB CDF
3. Vessel capacity: 35,343 dwt
4. Goods handled: Cruise passengers, containers, ro-ro, dry and liquid bulk, timber, coal, oil, steel, fruit juice, grain
5. Origin of name: Old Welsh and Celtic "fort on the Taff"

Authority: Associated British Ports
Tel: (02920) 400500

Cardiff's prosperity as a port began with the 2nd Marquis of Bute, who opened the city's first dock (the Bute West Dock) in 1839, quickly followed by several other family-owned docks. In feathering their own nests by ensuring that all the coal and iron produced on their land was exported via the family docks in Cardiff, the Butes also ensured the future of the city itself, which soon became one of the busiest ports in the world. Sea-trade dwindled in the 1930s but the city has seen a revival since being made capital of Wales in 1955. The docks are operated by Associated British Ports, whose subsidiary, the Grosvenor Waterside Group, has redeveloped 100 acres of the harbour area, which is now home to shops, restaurants and Wales's premier hotel, the distinctive St David's Hotel & Spa (the white circle at the centre of the picture).

Cardiff International Airport (Rhoose)
12m s-w of Cardiff

1. Opened: RAF 1942, Civil 1954
2. Air transport movements (2000): 20,196
3. Passengers (2000): 1,519,920
4. Runways: 03/21 (1,119 m) & 12/30 (2,354 m)
5. Radio frequencies (MHz): 125.0 (tower)/125.85 (approach)

Operated by: Cardiff International Airport Ltd
Tel: (01446) 711111

Rhoose was built as an RAF base for Spitfire training but was only used for two and a half years before being abandoned in August 1944. The airfield was redeveloped as a civil airport from 1952–54, with the present terminal building and a lengthened runway following in 1972. The airport had a slight identity crisis, changing its name from Glamorgan (Rhoose) to Cardiff-Wales in 1978 and later changing again to Cardiff International (Rhoose). From 1991–93, British Airways built one of the world's largest hangars here, used for overhauling 747s – the hangar can take four 747s wingtip to wingtip.

Fishguard (Abergwaun)
Pembrokeshire

1. Ferry & fishing port
2. United Nations carrier code: GB FIS
3. Vessel capacity: 6 m draught, 160 m length
4. Port handles: Containers, ro-ro, general cargo
5. Origin of name: Old Norse "fish yard" (Abergwaun describes location at the mouth of the River Gwaun)

Authority: Stena Line Ports Ltd
Tel: (01348) 404406

An inscribed stone at Fishguard commemorates the last invasion of the British mainland, which took place nearby in 1797 when a party of French soldiers who had intended to seize Bristol were blown off course and landed at Carregwastad Point. It is said that the soldiers mistook the traditional stovepipe hats and red flannel dresses worn by a group of local women for the uniform of the British Infantry, and immediately surrendered. Modern Fishguard is the ferry terminal for Rosslare in Ireland, with a smaller harbour to the south for pleasure craft.

Holyhead (Caergybi)
Gwynedd

1. Seaport
2. United Nations carrier code: GB HLY
3. Vessel capacity: 190 m length
4. Traffic (per annum): c. 2.5 m passengers, 0.5 m cars, 0.05 m freight vehicles, 0.01 m coaches
5. Origin of name: "Holy headland" (Caergybi refers to St Cybi)

Authority: Stena Line Ports Ltd
Tel: (01407) 606775

Holyhead has been an active port since at least 2,000 BC, trading in axes from Ireland and, 500 years later, in Irish gold. Today the port still thrives on trade with Ireland, though now in the more mundane form of ferries and the Stena Line catamaran, which reaches Dun Laoghaire in less than two hours.

Larne
County Antrim

1. Seaport
2. United Nations carrier code: GB LAR
3. Vessel capacity: 9.6 m draught, 35,000 dwt
4. Traffic (2000): c. 0.32 m commercial vehicles, 0.16 m passenger vehicles, 0.7 m passengers, 4.6 m tonnes freight
5. Origin of name: Irish Gaelic "lands of Lathair's people"

Authority: Larne Harbour Ltd
Tel: (01574) 872209

Larne offers the shortest sea crossing to Great Britain from anywhere in Ireland, and sees 38 ferries arriving and departing each day to and from Cairnryan, Fleetwood and Troon, carrying ro-ro freight, passengers and cars.

121

Milford Haven
(Aberdaugleddau)
Pembrokeshire

1. Seaport
2. United Nations carrier code:
   GB MLF
3. Vessel capacity: 20 m draught
4. Port handles: Crude oil,
   petroleum products, liquefied gas (c. 35 m
   t/year)
5. Origin of name: Old English and Old Norse
   "sand fjord harbour"

   Authority: Milford Haven Port Authority
   Tel: (01646) 693091

Aberdaugleddau, the Welsh name for Milford
Haven, means "mouth of the two Cleddau",
referring to the East and West Cleddau rivers
on whose estuary the town stands. The port
was founded at the instigation of Sir William
Hamilton, and it was here that Nelson stayed
with him and Emma, Lady Hamilton, in 1801,
shortly before she became Nelson's mistress
and bore his daughter Horatia. Milford Haven
is the name of the port in the north-western
corner of the photograph as well as the body
of water that flows across the centre, one of
Britain's largest natural harbours with a
deepwater channel capable of accepting the
largest supertankers.

Pembroke Dock was built after the naval dockyard relocated here from Milford Haven, and is a separate entity from the historic town of Pembroke. The dockyard closed down in 1926, and Pembroke Dock is now the terminal for the Irish ferry.

Pembroke Dock (Doc Penfro)
Pembrokeshire

1. Seaport
2. United Nations carrier code: GB PEM
3. Vessel capacity: 10 m draught, 169 m length, 30,000 dwt
4. Port handles: General cargo, timber products, fruit & vegetables, feeds (c. 0.3 m t/year)
5. Origin of name: Celtic "end of the land"

Authority: Port of Pembroke
Tel: (01646) 683981

Newport (Casnewydd)
Newport

1. Seaport
2. United Nations carrier code: GB GWE
3. Vessel capacity: 10.5 m draught, 244 m length, 39,239 dwt
4. Port handles: Steel, coal, forest products, fresh produce, general cargo, scrap metal (c.1.5 m t/year)
5. Origin of name: Disputed – "new port" or "new market town" (from the Latin derivation of port, meaning town gate)

Authority: Associated British Ports
Tel: (01633) 244411

Newport originally grew up around the Roman fort of Caerleon, an area that now forms a northern suburb of the modern town. Spanning the River Usk is Newport's famous Transporter Bridge, built in 1906 to carry people and cars across the river without obstructing the shipping lane below – the bridge transports up to 100 people and six cars at a time in a carriage suspended beneath a 240 ft-high gantry.

Port Talbot
Neath Port Talbot

1. Industrial port
2. United Nations carrier code: GB PTB
3. Vessel capacity: 16.7 m draught
4. Goods handled: Iron ore, coal
5. Origin of name: "Talbot's port"

Authority: Associated British Ports
Tel: (01792) 650855

Another port named after the family that built it, the docks at Port Talbot (formerly Aberavon) were developed in 1834 by Christopher Rice Talbot of Margam Abbey to support the local iron and copper industries. The docks were extended in the late-19th century to handle coal, and in 1972 a deep-water harbour was added to handle bulk ore supplying the Margam and Abbey steel-works.

1. Port & resort
2. United Nations carrier code: Not listed
3. Features: Butlin's Starcoast World
4. Industries: Tourism
5. Origin of name: Welsh "salt water pool" (referring to the circular bay)

Tourist office tel: (01758) 613000

The resort of Pwllheli centres around the five-mile sweep of the sand and shingle South Beach. The town is also a popular base for sailing and sea-fishing, with a 400-berth marina in the harbour.

Swansea (Abertawe)
Swansea

1. Port
2. United Nations carrier code: GB SWA
3. Vessel capacity: 9.9 m draught, 198 m length
4. Goods handled: Steel, oil, chemicals, coal, aluminium, petroleum products, sand, gravel
5. Origin of name: Old Danish and Old Norse (place of) "Sweyn's sea" (Abertawe describes location at the mouth of the River Tawe)

Authority: Associated British Ports
Tel: (01792) 633000

Swansea developed as a mining and ship-building town, and by the beginning of the 18th century was Wales's largest coal port. The city became heavily industrialized during the ensuing century, particularly with plants smelting copper and other metals. The legacy of this industry is a six-mile stretch of factories, quays and industrial buildings that is slowly being redeveloped. Parts of the docks to the west have recently been converted into a marina.

Index